PRESERVED FOR GREATNESS

SYLVIA ETIM

authorHOUSE®

AuthorHouse™
1663 Liberty Drive
Bloomington, IN 47403
www.authorhouse.com
Phone: 833-262-8899

Published by AuthorHouse 09/14/2020

ISBN: 978-1-7283-7353-9 (sc)
ISBN: 978-1-7283-7351-5 (hc)
ISBN: 978-1-7283-7352-2 (e)

Library of Congress Control Number: 2020917431

Print information available on the last page.

CONTENTS

DEDICATION

I dedicate this book to all single parents who have survived the enormous task, and the struggles associated in raising their children alone. The story can only be told by you. Do believe however that Jesus is ever present and you will not die while nurturing the seed that God has given to you. As a woman who went through great adversity and emerged to fight for her destiny, I encourage you to rise up with boldness, fearlessness and tenacity, for life holds wonderful treasures you are yet to discover. God in His infinite wisdom has a greater purpose that no man understands. Reach out for the Word of God that changes all things. And rest in His love knowing, with Him, life is not over.

PREFACE

A beautiful, innocent young little girl, full of vigour and enthusiasm, brought up in the village by her grandparents knows life has great and wonderful opportunities before her. However, nothing prepared her for the overwhelming odds in her latter years. Life unfolded in different dimensions and this was compounded in the some poor choices that she made. Enveloped in total darkness, her life took a dangerous and downward spiral until the Light of the world appeared – the Lord and Saviour Jesus Christ. Holding tight and trying to solve problems with God, she plunged further into despair and suffered repeated cycle of losses and confusion. That person is ME.

Despite an instruction from my father in the Lord, the General Overseer of the Redeemed Christian Church of God to "listen to the Holy Spirit", I kept doing my own things sometimes seeking solution in emptiness, craving for a filth-filled and old lifestyle God was trying to wrench from my hands. However in a divine dramatic twist, God was still faithful when in November 2009, I started listening to INSIGHTS *for* LIVING, a morning Christian telecast on a Nigerian television station. This was my turning point.

This is my story. It is not a story of survival but a chronicle of the manifold mercies of God on a life that could have been senselessly wasted by the enemy. A life that has shown that God keeps His Covenant and His promises do come to pass even in the face of contrary circumstances and predictions of men. It is a testimony of the power in the revelation of the

Word that lifted me from the valley of hopelessness to become infinitely confident to be what God had destined me to be. At my resurrection, the voices of men become insignificant and God alone is enthroned and ALL PRAISE BELONG TO HIM.

FOREWORD

PRESERVED FOR GREATNESS is a captivating read from Sister Sylvia Etim. It is a testimonial of God's faithfulness, mercy and unfailing love towards her right from childhood.

God permits us to experience the same graces. For he saith to Moses, I will have mercy on whom I will have mercy, and I will have compassion on whom I will have compassion. So then it is not of him that willeth, nor of him that runneth, but of God that sheweth mercy. Romans 9:15-16

The call of destiny begins in God even before we are conceived in our mother's wombs. Before I formed thee in the belly I knew thee; and before thou camest forth out of the womb I sanctified thee, and I ordained thee a prophet unto the nations. Jeremiah 1:5

Despite contrary forces contending to shipwreck the purpose of God for our lives, God desires to manifest Himself on our behalf to bring us to the expected end he has determined. For I know the thoughts that I think toward you, saith the Lord, thoughts of peace, and not of evil, to give you an expected end. Jeremiah 29:11

Sister Sylvia's book highlights that life can be a journey of various challenges between the forces of good and evil, God and satan, life and death, truth and falsehood.

Her story highlights the fact that the results we attain in life are impacted by the choices we make.

Life presents varied issues that we face constantly and our understanding of the purposes for which they exist and our attitude towards them are important. The consequences associated with choices we make are practically presented here.

The Word of God is God Himself. It is ever living and active. It does not change with changing times and it never loses its power. Knowing the Word and rightly applying it to our circumstances produces dramatic positive changes. This is true irrespective of how far we might have drifted from the path of life carved out for us by God Himself. A willing and obedient heart ready to accept God's Word becomes a beneficiary of God's unlimited grace.

Sister Sylvia Etim has in this book chronicled God's presence in her life from childhood in Opobo Province in the present Akwa Ibom State in Nigeria.

The initial departure of her father and subsequently her mother to the United States in pursuit of the 'golden fleece' and her upbringing alongside her siblings by her grandparents in the village make interesting reading.

The emotional turmoil experienced at the departure of her parents tugs at one's heart as we read this text. The encouragement and positive impact of her grandfather who encouraged reading of the Bible, prayer times and development of her singing talents are also well captured and reflect the benefit of positive influences upon our lives.

Sister Sylvia's determination to proceed with her secondary school education beyond the village and it's dramatic moments reflect the steely nature of her young character.

Her varied life experiences as an unbeliever reflect the storms we sometimes experience. In the midst of the various challenges she experienced Gods faithfulness and began to see the unveiling of God's divine plan for her life.

Single parents, separated couples, divorcees, the jilted, the forsaken, the neglected, the abandoned, the confused, the misdirected, the needy and the hopeless will discover in this book that looking up to mere mortals for help almost always results to frustration, devastation, disappointment, disillusionment, disgrace and shame and alienates one from God's ultimate help. Thus saith the Lord; cursed be the man that trusteth in man, and maketh flesh his arm, and whose heart departeth from the Lord. For he shall be like the heath in the desert, and shall not see when the good cometh; but shall inhabit the parched places in the wilderness, in a salt land and not inhabited? Jeremiah 17:5-6

We are encouraged trust in the Lord with all our hearts and He shall satisfy our deepest needs and lead us to our destinies.

Sister Sylvia encourages those passing through very trying moments resulting from past mistakes to snap out of self blame and pity parties. She challenges us all to take our destinies in our hands and discover from God's Word the paths we are to tread.

Life's circumstances shape and mould us to His image. And we know that all things work together for good to them that love God, to them who are the called according to his purpose. For whom he did foreknow, he also did predestinate to be conformed to the image of his Son, that he might be the firstborn among many brethren. Romans 8:28-29

Since we are still standing after all past challenging and bitter experiences, we join Sister Sylvia in boldly declaring that by His grace, we indeed have been PRESERVED FOR GREATNESS.

Enjoy this.

Pastor Oluremi Morgan
Pastor-in-charge of the RCCG, Lagos Province 35

To my son

I have held you in my arms from birth and I am amazed at how so soon you have become a man. You have evolved into a handsome, intelligent, God fearing young man and all I can do is to praise God.

I remember the years you have clung to me with tears in your eyes begging me to stay with you, but because I was playing a dual role, I had to work so that we could survive. The things you saw me accomplish then were not by my ability but the grace of God.

Life has taught you to be strong, tenacious and independent. I have no doubt you will be a good leader, husband and father, performing better the role you never had the opportunity to experience. You have seen so much in life but you have come out better. I know you will teach your children the lessons learnt and most importantly lead them in the way of the Lord.

ACKNOWLEDGEMENTS

There are quite a number of people who have played some very significant role in the course of my writing this book. First of all, I give glory to God for the privilege of coming in contact with some materials from the great men of God who have walked with Him amongst them my Father in the Lord, Pastor Enoch Adeboye, various sermons and programmes I listened to and attended that have impacted my life enabling me to garner knowledge for this Book.

I want to acknowledge the love, support and encouragement of Don and Elizabeth Unachukwu, Eyamba Odeh, Adebimpe Aderemi and Abosede Abodunde.

Thank you Tolulope Fadare for your encouragement and for standing by me in this journey. I really appreciate you.

A very big thank you to a special sister, Lorna Idoko for your unflinching support for being there from the beginning of this project until its completion. We have come a long, long way.

Pearl Mormah, I sincerely appreciate you. Thank you for your prayers, the right words, and your support.

To my dear Carol Anyaegbunam, you never for a second doubted God's ability in my life especially when I embarked on this project. Thank you for your consistency and encouragement.

And to you Mariam Fagbemi, you devoted your special moments despite your busy schedule to attend to this project with much love and great respect.

Uto Ukpanah, you scrutinised every sentence and made this project your priority. You demanded the best because you believed in me, thank you.

To Seyi Ladega, thank you so much for your support, your love and encouragement. I appreciate you.

And finally, thank you Mr. Sylvester Mbamali - your insight and mastery at translating thoughts and ideas I could not readily articulate significantly took the whole project to a new level. You refused to see the emptiness but rather saw the promises of God fulfilled in my life. Thank you for your sleepless nights, support, prayers and active participation in this project. I must say you epitomise excellence. Thank you sir!

Thank you and God bless you all.

Preserved for Greatness - REVIEW

I had the privilege and honour of reading through the manuscript for this book. *Preserved for Greatness,* catalogues the author's evolution in the circle of life that culminates in her ultimate connection to God.

Though I have known Sylvia for over 16 years, nothing prepared me for the revelations regarding her journey to self-discovery that reads like the Nollywood movie script. In this book the author opens her heart to readers without reservation; sharing the experiences that opens a window and gives perspective as to why she is who she is today in a divinely inspired manner.

The author reminisces with great clarity, about her childhood with great fondness and innocence; transiting into adulthood with little or no family support; her struggles as an abandoned spouse and single parent, shaking her trust in people and questioning her spirituality. Coming out of years of self-denial and soul searching, Sylvia finally found and activated her God ordained purpose.

In barring her heart and life in *Preserved for Greatness*, the author has obtained the peace that comes with obedience to God's command.

Uto Ukpanah (Company Secretary, MTN Nig)

CHAPTER 1

NEW SHOES, NEW SHOES

New shoes, new shoes,
Red and pink and new shoes
Tell me, what do you choose
If they did let us buy new shoes, new shoes
Red and pink and new shoes............

1968. I recall this nursery rhyme with childish delight and nostalgia. However, the author and title of this little poetry book I do not recall. It was a mini poetry book which contained many poems. Amongst the poems in the book, this is the most memorable. Over the years, it has been alive in my heart. This was a popular poem- turned song and it became very popular in the entire household and neighborhood In 1965, my father had gone in search of the "golden fleece". In those days, it was a big deal in the community when a man or a woman went to study abroad. It was expected that with that education, he/she would return and train his immediate and extended family members. My father had a scholarship and he left behind his very young wife (my mother) with five tender children (four girls and a boy). We were to learn later that the reason my father did not take us or even intended that we joined him in the United States was because he was afraid we would imbibe the western culture and probably refuse to follow him back to Nigeria. Being the first son in a polygamous home, it was a taboo in his community to relocate abroad with his children. The reasoning was that his inheritance would be gone forever. And that was the belief my dear father shared with his people.

A small village called Asong in the Opobo Province of the then South Eastern State of Nigeria is now called Mkpat Enin Local Government Area of the present Akwa-Ibom State in Nigeria. This is my mother's village, a predominantly Catholic community. I had started singing from the age of six and my mother had noticed that I had great interest in dancing, singing and memorizing nursery rhymes and could turn these poems into songs effortlessly. This became my main preoccupation and I was a very happy child. I had an after-school choral group comprising children from the neighbourhood and this was coordinated by my maternal grandfather. He loved me and always supervised my singing lessons.

My mother was a teacher and when her husband left, she moved to her parent's home in the village where she continued teaching. We lived with my grandparents, uncles, aunts, cousins, and other extended family members. My mother was posted to various stations and my grandmother always insisted that she left me behind. And I ended up being with her always when my mother would be in her various out stations with my siblings. My grandparents and parents were devout Catholics and we accepted no other expression of faith. I have no vivid recollections of my father's influence because I didn't really know him well. Much of what we learnt was from this environment.

I have very fond memories of my grandfather. I do not know how old he was then but he did not look old and he was a good man. We his grandchildren used to call him Tete. Very quiet and unassuming, a man of few words, he had a way of instilling discipline in us. He had a fragile cane which he used occasionally when all efforts to make us obedient failed. He was very slow in judgment, listening to all sides when there were issues.

My grandmother on the contrary was very bold and outspoken. She had seven children and was quite rich especially in relation to a local environment where wealth was measured by possession of farm lands, herds of domestic animals and palm trees. She was a giver and just loved to give people things. She gave out food, money and materials. She had people working for her in her farmlands. She would beat us mercilessly when we did wrong. I preferred Tete. This was our home

My grandfather read the Bible religiously. He would gather us to tell us stories and folktales. He encouraged us to continually go for church confessions (just in case we had "sinned") and participate actively in other church activities. Tete always led the morning and evening prayers. He made village life very interesting for us and instilled in us good morals and values. We were expected to greet and be courteous to people at all times and never to visit or accept anything from anyone no matter who it was. We strictly complied with these instructions.

> *Train up a child in the way he should go; and*
> *when he is old, he will not depart from it*
> *(Proverbs 22; 6)*

Tete taught us to read and memorize some Bible passages and Psalms, my favourites being Psalms 1,3 and 23. Those psalms have been etched in my memory since childhood. I never heard him curse or swear. If any of us used the name of God inappropriately, we were sure to be punished. My grandfather detested lying and would always mete out punishment. Anytime he felt that the cane did not have an impact on us, he would ask us to go to the stream and fetch water. Attendance at church services and other church activities, morning and night prayers was compulsory for everyone.

My most memorable moments were during the moonlight seasons. Tete would gather all of us and the children from the neighbourhood for story telling sessions. The folklores and the songs captivated us and evoked different emotions. We never got tired and never wanted these stories to end but they always ended so that everybody could return to their respective homes and retire to bed. These were very exciting and entertaining periods for me. We believed that the tortoise could talk, birds could sing and carry messages and animals could actually play human roles. We would dance, clap and sing. Festive periods like Christmas, Easter and New Year's Day were even more interesting. At Christmas time especially, the change in weather heralding the harmattan season would bring the entire family together where my grandfather would make bonfire and we would gather round and warm ourselves.

A trait I had developed while I was with Tete was reading especially at night while others were asleep. He encouraged me and would light the kerosene lantern for me and seat me comfortably. My grandfather took particular interest in my school work and helped me do my assignments. He had a pet-name for me, Mboso-Owo, (a rhetorical name meaning what have I done to someone?) No one else called me by that name. One constant and hilarious habit he had which we the grandchildren enjoyed making fun of, was his farting habit. If it was loud, we would all run to him and tell him, "Oh Tete sorry" repeatedly and he would nod his head in response and appreciation. We would thereafter laugh at him behind his back. Although he never caught us laughing at him, I'm sure even if he had, he would have been indifferent.

I loved to read story and poetry books and act out some drama. I also loved to write. I was so involved in these that everything else was secondary. I either had my books, and my songs or nothing else. My grandfather and I read books together and he became my instructor. I would spend most nights reading, practicing dance steps and composition of songs. The following day, I would be ready for school. Tete also noticed that certain things were different about me especially my resolve to excel in whatever I embarked on. My teachers marveled at my skills and they loved me. Any day I wasn't in school, they would come to the house to ask my grandfather the reason for my absence.

> *Listen, O isles, unto me and hearken, ye people from far; The Lord hath called me from the womb; from the bowels of my mother hath he made mention of my name. And he hath made*

*my mouth like a sharp sword; in the shadow
of his hand hath he hid me, and made me a
polished shaft: in his quiver hath he hid me;
And said unto me, Thou art my servant, O
Israel, in whom I will be glorified.(ISAIAH
49 : 1-3)*

On a typical day when I returned from school, I would meet my grandfather who would be seated on the front porch. Without removing my school uniform or caring if there was food for me to eat or not, I would simply bring out my book and settle down with him to continue from where I stopped the previous day or night. Thereafter, I would tell him I was ready to sing. Before long, he would have gathered a few children and we would begin to sing and dance.

My life continued in this idylic manner until my mother left to join my father. Little did I know that things would take a dramatic turn.

It was just a question of time.

CHAPTER 2

MOTHER EAGLE TAKES TO FLIGHT

My father left us in 1965 to the United States. My mother had told us how he left and how his family had come out to bid him goodbye. He was a primary school teacher and later headmaster of several primary schools in and around the community. We learnt he was very strict and disciplined. I could not really assess him at that age but before he left, I was seeing a picture of a man who was stuttering dramatically and occasionally, I could hear echoes of his angry stammering voice. He did not influence me in any way because I did not really know him. My grandfather was my father figure because I spent my childhood years with him.

My mother was always crying, and I did not know why. I guess the thought of leaving her children was so heavy on her mind. I never knew the implications then. She was preparing for her trip but refused to disclose to us except to her parents. She bought our books, clothes, everything and anything that would make all of us comfortable. She even organized domestic helps that would take care of us under the supervision of my grandparents. Everything looked set or so it seemed!

One morning after the usual morning prayers, we discovered our mother was gone. "Where is mother?" we asked. My mother was so grieved that she couldn't bear to announce her departure to us, so while we all slept, she had said a quiet goodbye, and with tears streaming down her face, departed.

Our parents were both gone. Well, we comforted ourselves; grandfather was there but would things remain the same? I clung to him. Would my mother's absence make much difference? Time would later reveal! Things were happening very fast. The domestic helps who were supposed to be responsible for us were busy with everything else except for us. They had forgotten their primary responsibility; they were to help prepare food, fetch water, and help us to get to school early. We however, did not have enough sense to complain. We quickly adjusted and got accustomed to our new way of life. Our parents were not there for us anymore. My parents were writing letters to us but on receipt, we would not open until we took it to Tete who would read out the contents to us.

My mother sent us clothes regularly especially during festive seasons. We were obeying the rules of the house so that Tete would allow us go to the village square to watch traditional displays of masquerades during Christmas. Sometimes, he forbade us because he felt the circumstances surrounding those displays were demonic. Some of those masquerades looked wild and wicked with sharp machetes and other dangerous weapons. They were frightening. At night, I would have nightmares in which these masquerades would appear pursuing me. I would report to Tete and would consciously stop visiting the square. These dreams continued irrespective of the season. When I shared them, we would all laugh but I was particularly troubled that I was never able to run when pursued in those dreams.

One regular feature in the household was my grandmother's affiliation to native doctors. She loved her children and in the quest to protect one of her daughters who was not faring well educationally, she sought solution from them. She granted them unlimited access to the house where they would perform and conduct various rituals about which we had no understanding.

This particular aunt of ours had tried unsuccessfully to complete her secondary school education. Her name was 'Ufen' which means 'suffering'. I do not know if my grandmother experienced extreme pain or stress when pregnant with her. And oh! my aunt suffered and

7

experienced so much pain and affliction. It had not dawned on anyone then (not even Tete who was always reading the bible) to envisage the consequences and gravity of his daughter bearing such a name. Yet she bore it with shameful dignity as she struggled with the futility of trying to make meaning out of her life.

Different weird-looking men visited, each performing different ritual sacrifices to deliver my lovely aunt who at this time had become accustomed to these strangers and their practices. Chicken after chicken and sometimes goats were slaughtered and in most cases, blood sprinkled. Sadly, her situation only appeared to worsen. As children, we found some of those rituals very comical. Sometimes, they were done at night or behind closed doors. Sometimes, we were fast asleep. Sometimes, childish instincts would arouse our curiosity causing us to stay awake and listen or peep through the key hole. Nevertheless, my grandmother was undaunted. She was determined that her daughter would go to school and like other young girls, pass her examinations. Curiously, although Tete never participated in any of these rituals, he also never questioned the presence of these strangers in his house despite the fact that some of them stayed for extended periods at a time. He either simply did not seem to notice what was going on or he deliberately turned a blind eye and just kept his mouth shut. In any case, his attitude towards these practices did not diminish my affection for him.

Somehow, I became the little star in the family. I was doing very well in school and I received many commendations. My after-school singing classes were progressing and I composed more songs. On the other hand, the domestic chores seemed to be intruding into my choral time but when ordered to go to the farm, I obeyed. I would leave and by the time we would return from the farm, it would be so late that I could only hide and cry, wishing for the day to break so that I could go to school, return and do my singing the following day. Sometimes, when we returned late from the farm, my grandfather would be waiting for us outside and he would express his displeasure with us for returning late. My grandmother would not be bothered. She could sometimes decide when I could go to school and when to stay back for farm work. I was not too bothered about the physical activities but I was feeling the pain of either missing school or my chorals. Yet my grandfather couldn't do anything.

One day, I returned from school excitedly looking forward to seeing my grandfather so that I could do my usual singing. I would usually sit outside with him to avoid Grandma. I had never been interested in other things because I had a passion that superseded hunger. Music, poetry, dance and drama were my preoccupation. But this day, he was not around so I still sat outside waiting for him and hoping he would return soon. As I settled down with my books, one of my aunts came and ordered me to go and do chores. It was apparent my hobbies had become a pain not only to my grandmother who had complained about the time I was spending on them. I cried and told my aunt I did not want to eat and that I wanted to be left alone to do my singing. Instantly, she seized my school bag, removed all the literature, poetry and drama books my mother had bought for me and ran inside while I ran after her crying, begging and pleading. I thought she was merely going to hide the books with a warning or she would be kind enough to keep them until Tete returned. I was wrong! She ran to the pit toilet and dumped all my books inside. I was devastated. I was barely nine years old. If the purpose was to silence me, she had succeeded momentarily. Unfortunately, my passion was so engraved in my spirit and even though I had cried so much, somehow, I knew deep down that my singing was not over. The days and months that followed were lonely. As usual, when I reported the matter to Tete, he comforted me. I had no books to read anymore, I was sad. I could not write and tell my parents for fear of being reprimanded. I felt locked up inside every day, wishing to explain myself. My enthusiasm, my excitement was gone. I had nothing to occupy myself with except the house chores which I had fully settled down to. I would still sit by my grandfather and he would tell me stories, I would still sing but with subdued tone. The children were no longer coming.

I clung to Tete with tears. My world had come crashing down. All I held unto, everything I loved to do, even the songs I composed were in the most unholy place of the earth where only maggots could hear the heart-broken cries of my silent voice. I would lie down on the bed and imagine myself singing, acting or dancing. I would hear loud applause and shouts from the crowd. I would imagine the audience demanding an encore and suddenly as if in a trance, I would awaken with tears in my eyes. I was barred from all I loved to do. I felt like a bird in a cage, singing through and flapping her wings but unable to escape. I vowed I would never stop singing.

By the time I was in primary six, it was quite evident that my grades had deteriorated. My teachers advised Tete to urge my grandmother to reduce the amount of chores. That was the only logical explanation they could give to my progressive disengagement. They felt I needed more time to catch up with my school work. I cannot remember if this instruction was adhered to.

Late one afternoon in school, I received a letter from my father. I cannot remember the contents but one sentence stood out. He said he would like me to repeat primary six so that I would do better in the secondary school. Maybe, the report of my decline had reached him. This was another blow to what I was already experiencing. Why would he ask me to repeat a class, I asked myself? I was angry and I took a pen and tried to delete it so that Tete would not see what was written. I took the letter home to Tete, my heart pounding, saddened and grieved. He opened and read it and saw where I had crossed the sentence but he was able to see what was written. Tete read the letter and said "Your father wants you to repeat primary six so that you can do well in secondary .... I interrupted without allowing him to finish and for the first time, I shouted at him and exclaimed an emphatic " NO". I told Tete I would rather die than repeat and I promised to do better in school. I started crying and begged him to kindly stand by me and also persuade my father to allow me continue instead of repeating. Though I forgot to ask him to keep this information away from my grandmother; I thought we had reached a compromise. To my utter amazement a few days later, my grandmother told me that she had heard what my father had said, so, I should not bother taking the Common Entrance Examination as it was known then. I was crushed. If my grandmother was in the know, then I should as well forget it. It was our practice to discuss our parents' letters and this particular letter was no exception. I wish Tete had kept this matter to himself.

When my class teacher bought a copy of the state newspaper to show us the advertisement for the Common Entrance Examination into secondary schools, I was distraught but pretended all was well and I went home. I waited for an appropriate time when I could talk to Tete alone. The time came and I told him that I needed some money to collect the form (the class teacher was mandated by the headmaster to collect money and get the forms for each pupil and get them filled and returned). This time around, he would keep my confidence. He gave me the money and the following day, I quickly collected the form, filled and returned it to my class teacher. Still, I was scared. I took the entrance examination. Back in the days, names of successful candidates were published in the newspapers. I passed. I still wasn't excited because my grandmother was the issue. My three choices were for an all-girls' Catholic institutions. The first choice was one of the best girls' schools at that time. Every parent wanted their little girls to be there. The school, Cornelia Connelly College was a Catholic and missionary school and it was renowned for the standard of discipline and academic excellence. I desperately wanted to be there. The date for the interview had been communicated to me.

In the meantime, I was more concerned about how I would get transport money to travel for the interview. The school located in the present day capital of my state of origin – Uyo, was quite a distance. My mother's elder brother lived in Uyo but I had never visited him. He was the one who brought things for us from my parents. But I had to act very fast because I did not have time on my hands anymore. And like I had vowed, I was not going to repeat primary six. I had no fears where Tete was concerned and I went to him. He agreed to give me transport fare for the trip.

For He shall give his angels charge over thee to keep thee in all thy ways. (Psalm 91:11

That night I couldn't sleep. I stayed awake for fear of being caught by my grandmother who did not know my plans. The interview was in two days time. I had to get to Uyo the following day so I could prepare for the interview the next day. The moon was shining so bright that I had mistaken that to mean the dawn of day and so I ran out quietly and hurriedly since Tete had already given me the money. I didn't tell Tete and I walked on to a place where I was told I would get a vehicle. I walked on but saw nobody for a distance of about four kilometers approximately. I was not afraid. That route was not habitable, it was all bushes and a thick forest before reaching the junction of the town. I was walking and running so that I could catch the first vehicle. I finally got to the place and I waited a while, but when I didn't see any sign of any vehicle or human being, I started running back home. When I reached home, I tapped Tete's window and quietly called him out. He opened the window and asked what I was doing outside. When I told him, he was shocked! He checked the clock and told me that it was just few minutes after 2 am. He opened the door and asked me to go to sleep and assured me he would wake me at dawn. Unfortunately, I slept off and by the time I woke up, it was already morning. Tete had forgotten to wake me up. I was desperate. I ran out immediately to the same destination but by the time I got there, I learnt the vehicle had left and there would not be another vehicle until the following day which was the day of the interview. I ran back to tell Tete weeping all the way home.

As I approached the house, I met a young man who was a frequent guest at our house and he asked me why I was crying. After opening up to him, he told me not to cry and he offered to collect Tete's bicycle and take me back while assuring me that I would find another vehicle to Uyo no matter how late. When we got home, Tete obliged; thankfully and pumped the two tyres of his bicycle and handed it over to the good Samaritan and we left. I got a vehicle which took me to Uyo.

CHAPTER 3

FAMILY RE-UNION

I will instruct thee and teach thee in the way which thou shalt go: I will guide thee with mine eye. (Psalm 32:8)

When we reached Uyo, the driver announced "This is Uyo and this is the final bus-stop". He must have noticed that one of his passengers was not a seasoned traveler because I had been anxiously looking out of the window since the territory was unfamiliar. I disembarked from the bus armed with the address of my uncle's house.

My uncle was the regional manager of Dunlop Industries, in the South East zone at that time. He used to make monthly visits to the village and communicated more regularly with my parents. His arrival was always marked by shouts of joy because we knew that he would come laden with gifts from my parents. As I was walking down the street, I didn't see any street name or number. Instinctively I decided to stop by a beautiful storey building to ask for directions. The man I approached told me the address I was looking for was the house I had entered and the man I wanted to see lived upstairs. I was relieved to realize I had found my way to my uncle's house.

By 8am the following day, we were at Cornelia Connelly College. The school was big with well- manicured lawns, nice looking dormitories, big classrooms and beautiful offices. The Reverend Sisters were Irish and immaculately dressed in white with their veils and rosaries hung around their necks. I longed to be a part of this great institution.

Parents had brought their children so beautifully dressed for this interview. They came from all over the country. I met two girls from my class who were also successful. We exchanged greetings but I noticed they were looking at me oddly. Then I realised why I was such a wonder: I had no shoes on and they laughed but I had carried an umbrella and an old rainproof boot that my mother had left behind. It was not raining so I didn't wear them. I do not know what happened to the shoes my mother bought for me. But that was not the issue. They could laugh as much as they wanted, I knew what I wanted.

It was evening and suddenly, an announcement was made that those who came from distant States and other far locations be given preference so they could return before nightfall. There was a general disagreement from the parents and in the ensuing confusion, the door to the interview room was left half open and a security guard was placed at the door to prevent further disorder. At this point, I started shaking all over because the chances of my getting in was remote as parents had become very agitated and wanted to force their children in. But I was watching so intently because by this time I had positioned myself near the entrance door. My attention was on the girl in front of the panel of interviewers, and I noticed that the candidate was almost standing up when I quickly bent under the security man's hands and dashed and sat in front of the panel. They welcomed me and were very polite. Outside were screams and struggling and pushings. Then the Reverend sisters advised that the door be shut. At that point, I knew I would not be bundled out.

Less than one month later, my grandfather had a surprise visitor with a letter. It was a congratulatory letter of admission into the school I had so much dreamed of. My grandmother at this time knew I was resolute but I was still not talking except to Tete and my uncle. I immediately wrote to my father about my successes in my Common Entrance Examination and my interview, promising him that I would do well in the secondary school. My uncle on the other hand had promised that he would pay my school fees and purchase all I needed.

It was on one of our usual trips to the farm and about six o'clock in the evening when we heard the unusual sound of gun shots. At first, we dismissed it but it became louder and more rapid and my grandmother was concerned. We kept on working, and shortly afterwards, we heard footsteps and shouts calling on all of us to leave the farm immediately and return home. What had happened? My parents had returned from the United States. What ecstasy! It was unbelievable! I cannot remember taking any of the farm tools. My siblings ran wildly, shouting sometimes, falling down and getting up to go fall into my parents' warm embrace. I was happy but I did not still know my father's position on my admission since I did not get a response from him before he returned. But the fact that they were back was enough cause for celebration. At least we would no longer be subjected to hard labour. In keeping with the custom of the day, my parents were welcomed back with fanfare to celebrate my father's successful completion of his education in America. We were very excited and we couldn't sleep. We stayed up all night plying them with questions and trying to talk about everything all at once. Our new found freedom was so evident. Truly, Moses had come to take the children of Israel out of Egypt, we chorused.

My father who had obtained a Masters Degree in History from Lincoln University did not waste time getting a job as a teacher and subsequently as a school principal. By this time, he had relocated us. They got me ready for secondary school. Curiously though, in spite of the fact that I was passing my exams in primary school, I had noticed a decline that I could not understand and found it very hard to explain. I found it difficult to ignite that fire but things still looked normal. I couldn't tell my parents because I couldn't explain what the matter was. However, I embraced the new school and the new experience. I was close to the Reverend Sisters and they got to know my father who was always visiting. I still had great interest in literature and music. I joined the Glee club and I loved French language but owing to the lackluster French teacher, I struggled with it until I completely lost interest. At the time I was to pick subjects of interest, in my final year, my father insisted that I picked science subjects as he wanted me to become a medical doctor. I had excelled in the arts subjects. Science subjects were a no-go area except Biology. I struggled with Mathematics, Physics and Chemistry. I had no inclination to the medical sciences but my father had unfortunately imagined me with a stethoscope and doctor's overall. By the time I sat for the West African Examination Certificate (WAEC), and JAMB examinations it was obvious that as long as my interest was not there, I was wasting my time. Before I finished secondary school, I remember my father calling one day to request for permission from the school principal to take me away. My grandmother had died and my father wanted me to witness the funeral. The principal refused to let me go with him. My father had to leave without me. But I did miss her nevertheless.

When we reunited as a family once again, I noticed that my parents frequently had some form of misunderstanding. At some times, my father would express his frustrations in our presence. In a polygamous setting where the eldest and first son, my father, was expected to have many male children he had only one son and four female children while his brothers had numerous male children. My father had threatened at several times to take a second wife for this reason. All we could do was watch helplessly as my mother was riled and ridiculed by his people. His brothers had apparently fathered more male children and it did not matter what they became in life, as long as they were male children.

Despite their problem, my father actively lived up to his responsibilities as a father. Also, it was no secret that he took special interest in me and everything I would later do in life. My siblings and family attributed this to the fact that I resembled my father in all aspects. No wonder they called me his 'handbag'. Like him, I had also stuttered when I was much younger. The joy in the family was often punctuated by this gender issue. However, despite all his threats, my father never took another wife and we still remained a family.

After my West African School Certificate examinations in 1978, as was the practice then, the school principal would permit us to go out from school to return at a stipulated time. We had come of age, you might say. We had received so much discipline in the school that the thought of disobeying rules did not cross our minds. We had been taught basic etiquette. Also, sexual relations and dalliance with the opposite sex was not entertained in any way. In fact, it was a taboo to even discuss it. Any form of misconduct was brought to the attention of the school principal or the Reverend Sisters. Incidents of misbehavior were few.

On one of such outings, before our final departure from school, a friend and I had gone to eat in my uncle's house in town. Returning later in the evening, we passed through the then College of Education (now University of Uyo). It was a short route leading to our school. Oblivious of the people around us, two young male adults appeared from the back. One was by my side and the other by my friend's side and we exchanged pleasantries. The one by my side was slightly tall, dark and slim. He wore a pair of jeans and a sky blue shirt and was well mannered. Impressed by his boldness, we all got into a conversation and walked down some distance before they turned back and we got into school.

I would stop by to see him on my subsequent outings and we became friends. The relationship was new but totally platonic. I would tell my friends and my siblings and they would make fun of me. We would laugh and make jokes about my "new found love". And there was nothing more. On the final day of my departure, my father arrived to pick me up. As he drove through the gate of my very famous school, I looked back at the great institution that had molded me into a vibrant and promising young lady. I saw the College of Education where my platonic friend was and I wondered where he would be now. My father did not know what was in my mind. He was busy discussing with me. I had finished secondary school and would proceed to the University to continue my education. My relationship with the young man didn't progress further. But coincidentally, he had come to know my family through one of my aunts who was in the same institution with him. Our very few meetings were not planned and so we never really had much to talk about.

That relationship would not unfold until thirteen years later and would define the course of my life ushering in a storm that would set me up on the path to meeting my Lord and Saviour – The Lord Jesus Christ.

CHAPTER 4

THE GREAT ESCAPE

I finally got admission into the University of Calabar, Cross River State after three failed attempts to gain admission for Medicine after I had completed a higher school certificate education. A year later, I transferred to the University of Ibadan to study Language Arts. Thereafter, I was posted to do my National Youth Service Corps in the northern part of Nigeria, precisely Kaduna State. I was however undecided about working or pursuing a Masters degree program. For the meantime, I decided to take some time off and visit London in 1988 to enjoy the summer.

I boarded the then Nigeria Airways flight to Heathrow. The flight was to make a stop-over at Kano International airport and pick more passengers because it was a Boeing 747 with only a few passengers from Lagos. A young man from the Eastern part of Nigeria who had apparently spotted me while going through the immigration process and who was on the same flight came and sat with me. We started a conversation about various subjects, laughed and joked. I felt at ease probably because there were other people in the aircraft. He was so excited about his family and showed me their photographs and talked about a young lady he said he was marrying soon. As the plane landed, we disembarked. I needed to make a quick call and he advised that I should make the call in his room since he was checking into the Excelsior hotel at Heathrow. I agreed. Before I made the call, he had first made a call to a relation. After my call which lasted a few seconds, I said "Thank you" while carrying my bag to the door.

> ### *He that walketh with wise men shall be wise: but a companion of fools shall be destroyed. (Proverb 13: 20)*

I had barely spent three to four minutes in the room and I was heading to the door with my bag when Mr. Obiakor (not real name) apprehended me and requested that I stayed back. I politely turned down the request and explained to him that it was impossible for me to stay. By now, he had locked the door and took out the key. The once friendly and jovial person was becoming an angry and monstrous devil. Mr. Obiakor started confessing his love for me and the more I insisted on leaving, the angrier he got. Was this love? I didn't even have time to reason. Both of us were standing by the door. He went to his bag and brought out money and said "Here, take it for your shopping tomorrow, It is five thousand pounds sterling". I smiled and thanked him and refused to take it. He went and brought more money and added. Twice, I turned it down and Mr. Obiakor went wild. I stood in shock and disbelief. There was no way of escape. It would only take God to deliver me. But did I know this God? "I have already called my host, I insisted calmly". He swore he would not let me go and thereafter went to lie down on the bed with the key inside his trouser pocket. I stood by the door and got tired. He had slept for about an hour or so when he woke up suddenly to find me sitting down. This time he was more forceful. I told him I had stomach ache and it would be better for him to leave me in that position. In a fit of rage, he called the bar to bring a bottle of small stout. When the barman arrived, he did not allow him to enter, he quickly opened the door slightly and told the barman to go with the change and locked the door again.

> ### *He disappointed the devices of the crafty, so that their hands cannot perform their enterprise*

(Job 5:12)

Mr. Obiakor by now had removed his trouser and shirt except for his under pants. He insisted that I drank the stout because it would relieve me of my stomachache. He tried to force me to drink it but I was adamant. And he believed that if he didn't have his way then, he may probably never have so he went to bed and asked me to undress and join him. I started fiddling with my shirt buttons and my heart was racing while he was getting increasing impatient.

For with God, nothing shall be impossible
(Luke 1:37)

Mr. Obiakor was lying down on the bed waiting for me to undress and join him on the bed but my spirit was protesting no! Suddenly the telephone rang. This was the call he made immediately he entered the room and the person had promised to call him back. Mr. Obiakor was naked except for his pants. That he had made up his mind on what to do was not the issue. The issue was that no matter his intent and purpose, God had the ultimate say. Mr. Obiakor turned round to pick up his call. God had caused him after the barman left to lock the door and leave the key inside the lock and go back to bed. He forgot to take the key back into his pocket. And as he turned on to pick the receiver, my eyes went to the door, I unlocked it and I flew out like a flash of thunder.

If Mr. Obiakor had his trousers on, he would have caught up with me because the speed at which he pursued me shirtless and with trouser barely settling on him, it would have been a different story. God had also made him to undress because he could not run out naked. I did not know my way in the hotel but I just kept running. Then I saw a button and I pressed it and it opened and I entered. This man had almost reached the lift area and in less than a minute, the lift opened and before I knew it, I was on the ground floor. I had miraculously escaped. This ugly experience would set a parameter for my interaction with the opposite sex going forward. A seasoned Nigerian journalist who happened to be in London shortly after this incident and heard of it had privately taken up the matter and investigated him. He learnt Mr. Obiakor was a drug baron and was reputed to have a way with young beautiful women some of who lost their lives in mysterious circumstances. If all I heard were true, then my escape was divine.

I returned to Nigeria exactly one month later. Few months later, precisely in April 1989, I took up an appointment with the Corporate Affairs division in a big bank. I had decided to be on this job probably for one or two years, make some money before going back to school. I didn't have any passion for the job but I tried to like it and also apply myself.

There was something inside of me that was yearning for expression and I was ignoring it. I found the job too restrictive to my nature. But I kept at it and also kept my Catholic faith and was not in a hurry to change it. I was under close supervision of my immediate supervisor, a man of God, Mr. Omawunmi Michael Efueye, (popularly called Pastor O) a man of integrity and impeccable character, he was my official guardian in my place of work.

Every Monday morning in the office after my press reviews, one thing I did which nobody told me to do and which I had absolutely no explanations for was cutting out written sermons of the General Superintendent of Deeper Life Bible Church, Pastor W.F. Kumuyi, Presiding Bishop of Living Faith, Bishop David Oyedepo and the General Overseer of the Redeemed Christian Church of God, Pastor Enoch Adeboye from two national newspapers; Sunday Punch and Sunday Concord. I never read them but I kept these materials which proved useful to me decades later.

> ***Jesus answered and said unto him, Verily, verily, I say unto thee, Except a man be born again, he cannot see the kingdom of God. (John 3:3)***

This was the scripture that my guardian and immediate supervisor, Pastor O "pestered" me with. He repeatedly urged me to give my life to Jesus Christ and I did not find this funny and there were times I got angry. He was interceding for me and I never knew. One day, a top management staff walked in to see him. He looked at me and smiled. I smiled back. Then he looked at Mr. Efueye and gave a very powerful prophetic word concerning me. Oh! I got upset. Mr. Efueye noticed and grinned with smiles. As soon as the man left, I bared my mind. "Please tell your born-again friends never to look in my direction when they come to see you" I said angrily. Mr. Efueye had always laughed at me each time this "born-again" issue would come up. But I didn't forget a particular statement he constantly made. He had stated categorically that I should not worry and that there was no need for me to get angry, that God is waiting for me and when it is time, He would show up! I was haunted by this statement. I didn't want Him to show up, not so soon.

> *But the Lord said unto him, Go thy way for he is a chosen vessel unto me, to bear my name before the Gentiles, and kings and the children of Israel. For I will shew him how great things he must suffer for my name's sake. (Acts 9:15)*

Shortly afterwards, I came to know the management staff as Mr. Sylvester O. Mbamali, another devout Christian. Very calm and a man of great depth, he turned out to be the one I would run to for comfort when events in my life started unfolding.

Words had been spoken and the process through which God would catch my attention had been set in motion.

And there would be no hiding place for me.

CHAPTER 5

THE MARRIAGE OF LIKE -MINDS.

Ecclesiastes 3:14 I know that, whatsoever God doeth, it shall be forever: nothing can be put to it nor anything taken from it: and God doeth It, that men should fear before him.

The institution of marriage is as old as creation. The perfect God made it absolutely perfect. When people interfere with what God has ordained and introduce man-made ideas and manipulate it to suit them, it becomes perverted. Man has tried and failed woefully. But they have hung on pretending all is well when in fact all is not well.

God knew Eve would be a handful so He did not create more than one woman for Adam. Eve succumbed to the devil and thereafter contaminated Adam. The one that God had given responsibility to was taking instructions from the one that came out of him. If there were two women for Adam, the garden of Eden would have literally gone up in flames. Man has manipulated marriage so easily as if God did not know how to make it right. From the acquisition of wives and concubines, sometimes we embellish and give it other names: mistress, lover, friend, the list is endless. We arrange situations to suit us. And the sacredness of marriage loses its meaning. And God watches, not in admiration or approval but in holy justice as His children destroy themselves. We justify our actions because God does not have a wife and does not know how it feels to be rejected or abandoned. He knows the danger, he knows the consequences, He knows the pains, He knows the hurts. We hide under our culture, we justify from the bible. "After all, David who God loved had so many wives and concubines" And what about Solomon, we all ask? Still, God refuses to lower His standard.

A little above one year after I took on the job, I received a letter from the United States. I could not readily discern the handwriting as I had a few female friends over there. However, on opening, I found out that it was my platonic friend I had met after my final exams in my secondary school. He had written a five page letter and included his photograph. He told me how he got my address and how he had been looking for me over the years. I was very happy to hear from him again and with child-like enthusiasm, I decided to reply and keep the contact open. From the photograph, he had become more mature physically and so thirteen years later, we were back and no longer as kids. We were now communicating through the telephone and through letters. Mr. Efueye noticed my excitement and the long distance calls which were now very regular and he became very skeptical. I was adamant.

Proverbs 1:5; A wise man will hear, and will increase learning; and a man of understanding shall attain unto wise counsels

By 1991, he had paid me a visit. If I was happy, Mr. Efueye was not. He knew the danger of getting into a marriage on a very faulty foundation. Was this young man destined to be a part of the journey of my life? Pastor O knew I had no understanding and very importantly, he knew that the relationship was headed for the rocks as long as I did not have the Lord Jesus Christ as my foundation. If there were red signals when he came (and there were), I had approached them very casually.

Matthew 15:14; Let them alone: they be blind leaders of the blind. And if the blind leads the blind, both shall fall into the ditch.

25

If he found me strong-willed and stubborn, he made light of it. We were in a make-believe world. Both of us had no knowledge of the Lord Jesus Christ and it did not look as if we were in a hurry to do so. We were making progress in our relationship trying to talk and get some information about each other. My platonic friend was already in "an arranged green card marriage and was very miserable hence he had spent all the years looking for me". Those were his exact words. He said that was the reason he had to come personally to see me instead of talking about it over the telephone. He said he was already in the process of getting a divorce and that as soon as his arranged marriage was dissolved, we would get married. I continued with my job. We were communicating more frequently. It seemed life would hand me the best dreams ever. But was I right? On Saturday June 19, 1993 we had our traditional marriage. Traditional rites that I did not understand were performed and libation was offered. In my spirit, I knew something was not right. I was not happy. It was apparent that both of us were immature and were yet to come to terms with reality. Probably on my part, I needed a knight in shining armor, a messiah who would lay down his life for me. If my expectations were high, the thought of living with a husband was higher. I would later wake up to a very bad dream.

My now declared husband had plans but his plans were as far as he could think. They were not immediate plans. I would join him but it would not be immediate, it would not be in two or three or four years! He had rushed to marry me according to him so that another man would not take me away. My dear husband had made no plans for divorce. I instantly called off the marriage. He returned to America trying to salvage the situation but it was too late. I turned to the comfort of my family. By the time both families tried to mediate, it had gotten out of hand and the situation had caused a lot of animosity between the two families. My world was beginning to spin but I never envisaged it would spin so uncontrollably. Something was happening. My laughter had died.

I have heard many such things. Miserable comforters are ye all (Job16:2)

Accusations and counter-accusations filled the air. Gossips, unsolicited intermediaries were strategically positioned everywhere. There was chaos. Marital "counselors" tried desperately to offer their services. Friends were not left out. Family members felt they had the best solution. I even thought I could handle it myself. Confusion, confusion, all rolled into one. As I was trying to make sense of all the confusion, I fell ill and had so much discomfort in my sleeping pattern and other sensory organs. I started treating myself for malaria and I got worse and I was advised to go to the hospital. The doctor carried out a test and returned with a report – Pregnant! "Impossible" I screamed. I decided to terminate the pregnancy since I was not sure I could cope with it alone but for the timely intervention of a close female friend.

While the storm was raging, I continued with my office work. Mr. Efueye had come to terms with my decision and was convinced God would show up. He watched prayerfully as the tears were coming. Gradually, the pregnancy progressed. I was very sick during the first trimester and would only hold down peppers and alcohol in order to manage the nausea. I registered at the Lagos University Teaching Hospital. After the necessary tests were carried out, the doctor advised that I should get four pints of blood available as my blood level was very low. The diagnosis was not pleasant. It sounded very grim. I took the prescribed vitamins and contacted my husband about the pregnancy.

It was a difficult time.

CHAPTER 6

THE BIRTH IN A "MANGER"

The initial difficulties with the pregnancy reduced drastically after the first trimester and I felt better. On my various trips to the teaching hospital, I had met an old school mate, Liz who worked there and was an experienced nurse and midwife. She regularly checked on my progress. However, a few weeks before my expected date of delivery, the hospital staff embarked on an indefinite strike. The most natural thing for me to have done then was to have registered in another public or private hospital but I did not because I thought the strike would be called off soon. She had also instructed that if I felt or noticed anything unusual, I should report immediately. Throughout the pregnancy period, except for the usual symptoms ranging from nausea, sleeplessness, loss of appetite, repulsive sensory discomforts, I did not experience any serious health crisis. I was normal and my stomach did not protrude. By the time people noticed my pregnancy, I was far gone.

On Sunday March 28, 1994, 2.14am I suddenly awoke with very excruciating pains in my abdomen. Unable to fathom what could have caused such and oblivious of the fact that I had been given March 28 as my expected date of delivery, I got up from the bed. I was completely wet as I had fallen into labour without knowing. I dressed up and waited till the early hours of the morning when I drove first to the office and later to the hospital.

> *And she brought forth her firstborn son, and*
> *wrapped him in swaddling clothes and laid*
> *him in a manger, because there was no room*
> *for them in the inn (Luke2:7)*

The midwife's first reaction on examining me was that of complete shock. Reason? I was fully dilated. She immediately took me to a good hospital in the area. I was rejected because the hospital did not have my medical history and file and they did not want to be held responsible if anything went wrong. We got the same response from another hospital. By this time, the pain was unbearable. It is common practice among professional government workers to do some private practice. A male doctor in the Teaching hospital had a private hospital and the midwife decided to take me there. Nothing suggested that it was a hospital when we eventually located the place. It was a tiny room with a small reception area. There was only one staff, an auxiliary nurse. There were two tiny beds tucked into the room. This "hospital" was in a compound that housed many other business apartments and mini rooms. As we entered the room, we were greeted by lizards, geckos and other pests running to take position. There were cobwebs all over the room. The midwife hurriedly got a broom and tried to make the place look habitable. Fortunately, she had carried along some of her medical aids. By 11 am, we had settled in and I had the most excruciating pain one could ever imagine.

It was torture. I had cried so much that I didn't have the strength to cry anymore. I was lying down on the bed, the slim mattress was on a bed whose springs had weakened and so my back was sunk into the mattress and this position did not help my back. My crying had attracted a whole lot of the residents because they were living there. Some peeped through the only window that was the room. A friend we met on the way to this hospital was with us and she and the auxiliary nurse were bombarding the gates of heaven with their prayers. I was shouting with the little strength I had left and I was gradually drifting off. But I would be awakened with some mild slaps on my cheeks. Four hours later or thereabout, a man came in. I learnt he was the owner of the "hospital".

He put on his gloves, inserts his hands and shakes me vigorously and leaves. I was almost dead. Pain! I wanted to die.

At about 7 pm when the sun set, the room was in darkness because the room had no electrical bulb so candles were bought and an old lantern lit. A small crowd had gathered. They knew it was serious because I had been crying since morning. The baby had not descended into a birthing position. The lantern was still being pointed to the position where the baby was going to come out from. The midwife had not given me episiotomy because my stomach was very small and she thought the baby might be small too. I cried for death to come. It didn't come. Liz was composed. If she was afraid, she didn't show it but it was a life and death situation for her. Two lives were on the line and all she needed was God's intervention. She joined in the prayers. The whole atmosphere was dark except for the candles and the lantern. The prayers drowned the voice of my wailings.

And the heavens opened. And God heard. He didn't hear my cries. He didn't hear my wailings or groaning. He didn't hear my pleas for He is not moved by emotions. He heard the name of Jesus and He arose because Jesus has shed His blood for me. The baby's head had not engaged even at this point and suddenly something happens. The mercy of God was about to speak!

At about 9:47 pm or thereabout, my system was threatening to explode and I told the midwife. I felt a mad rush downwards and I saw the midwife trying to take position. She had done this a hundred times but I didn't know that this was the moment! In five minutes what came out sent shock and wild shouts of jubilation by onlookers who had by now milled around. The street is agog. The baby comes out in a flash and weighed between 4.2 – 4.4 kilogram. There is no weighing machine but the midwife from her long years of nursing and midwifery gives the estimation. A male child! He cannot be carried on open palms like other newborn babies. He has to be held to the shoulder because he is very huge. I had a third degree tear and had lost sensation from my neck downwards, only that I was alert mentally. The midwife stitched and dressed me up. She spent some time and left. Later in the night, a sick and deranged woman is brought into the other bed on admission. She looked awful. I cannot remember if I was able to sleep especially as I could not lift up myself. There was no blood transfusion. By morning, I had regained consciousness of my entire body and except for the stitches, I was well and strong. God had shown Himself strong and mighty. The union had produced a seed that would give me joy for the rest of my life. There were no male hands to welcome the child except the hands of those God had destined to do so. The following day, Mr. Efueye came, carried the baby and prayed for him and left.

A few hours later, I took my baby home …….

Alone.

CHAPTER 7

THE CALL

My son was born under some miraculous circumstances yet I still did not know this God that was behind this miracle. My focus was on the issue on the ground. A new year had come and nothing was different. I was however beginning to learn some lessons, especially the fickleness and the frailties of the human heart. The real life was beginning to unfold. I would learn some very shocking new lessons. When my mother-in-law came to stay with us in Lagos to procure a visa to the United States to visit her children, a particular couple (who were my husband's cousin and his wife) had called me and advised me to do the unthinkable because they said she was evil. That was strange. There was so much pressure and so much intrigue. I had discussed this with my cousin who lived with me at the time and she restrained me. The devil was ready to conscript me into his army and I never knew. Tempers were still running high. Meanwhile, my son was growing gracefully.

I had allowed the whole world entry except one man – Jesus. I had listened to all but One. And then one afternoon during a lunch hour fellowship led by Mr. Efueye, I finally gave my life to Christ. That was 1996. Oh! such peace, such joy! Sins forgiven, blood-washed, grace multiplied. I had become the righteousness of God in Christ. A completely new creature, the life of God was imparted to my spirit, recreated, born again! I now had the Father, Son and the Holy Spirit residing in me. Whether I would allow Him play a Father's role in my life would be another issue. It was not the end of the crisis but it was the beginning of a new life, a new experience altogether, on a very new level. Few years later, Mr. Efueye left Nigeria for a ministerial duty in London as a pastor in House on The Rock church for the next seventeen years.

> *Therefore if any man be in Christ, he is a new creature, old things are passed away; behold all things are become new. (2 Corinthians 5:17)*

I started attending The Redeemed Evangelical Mission and enrolled in the Believer's Foundation classes and got water baptized. Then I started reading faith books by late Rev. Kenneth E. Hagin and got materials that would help me advance spiritually. I thought as soon as one was born-again, every issue I faced would automatically be settled. So I became more focused on what I wanted than surrendering completely to Jesus and asking for His Will to be done in my life.

I was now a born-again Christian. I had seen the excitement on the faces of Christians and was hearing great testimonies. I therefore thought my decision would translate into an automatic release of miracles from heaven and the puzzle of my life solved. This was a huge joke. Or, probably since I had messed up a lot, God expected me to undo them before He could come on the scene, my joke. The stress of caring for a child alone had hit me and I resolved to write back to this young man, apologise and see where we could mend the fractured relationship. I did not have any experience of motherhood, worst of all single parenting. But the more I attempted to do things my way, the messier it got and the more frustrated I became. And the more the forces against me became stronger.

One Sunday, a friend invited me to a parish of The Redeemed Christian Church of God and the word preached had impacted my spirit. But whether I would stay with that word was another story. That experience however began my membership of the Redeemed Christian Church of God.

I didn't know that I had a date with the Ancient of Days. And He wasn't in a hurry to be stampeded. Who can stampede Him anyway? I would have to know that I am the bride that the groom wanted to show to the world and for this I would have to get prepared.

The journey was about to begin. The groom was waiting and I had taken the first step.

CHAPTER 8

I BELIEVE IN DREAMS AND VISIONS

I was beginning to enjoy my new found faith altogether. Before I joined the Pentecostal church, I never knew how to study the Bible. Except the few psalms I memorized as a child, I had no revelation. I also believed that praying and receiving answers was an exclusive preserve of a selected few. At least, I could go to the prayer champions and they would pray for me, I reasoned. That was the level I was operating on. The same applied to the study of the Word.

> *But Naaman was wroth, and went away and said, Behold, I thought, He will surely come out to me, and stand, and call on the name of the Lord his God, and strike his hand over the place, and recover the leper. (2 Kings 5: 11)*

I was getting acquainted with the church programmes especially the monthly Holy Ghost services. I had started hearing and reading about the great miracles that were being recorded at those services. Before I started worshipping with the Redeemed Christian Church of God, I had some visitations from the General Overseer, Pastor Enoch Adeboye in my dreams. I did not understand the dreams but noted them nevertheless. Now, I was under his authority, I reasoned that probably God wanted me to see him so I sent a few letters detailing my challenges. A response from one of the letters got me confused and frustrated. The man of God advised that I should listen very carefully that the Holy Spirit will speak to me, and that he was also praying for me. "Holy Spirit, speak to me"? "How will He speak, what language will he use, when and where? I questioned myself. Why did he not tell me what the Holy Spirit would say? Questions, questions, questions and very ignorant questions! Exasperated, I stopped writing and that declaration would haunt me for years. The stress of the job, and playing a double role to a child was weighing heavily on me and all my attention was on a relationship that should not have been in the first place. My attitude, emotional well-being and relationships were affected. That was the vicious cycle I found myself year after year.

I do not know if people pray to dream, have visions or experience trances or even hear voices. I never did. I have however prayed for the gifts of the Spirit as I was maturing spiritually because the Bible instructs us to do so. Even though I was learning to grow in the things of the Lord at this time, I knew one could fall into error if one tried to force or manipulate spiritual things, like wanting to hear a voice or experience some other spiritual manifestations. On the night of March 13, 1996, I had a very strange dream. As soon as I woke up, I took a notebook and wrote down the details. That was the start of my dream journaling till date. God had been faithful. He gave me the privilege to pick up some things in the spirit. Things that the physical eyes could not see. Amazingly, 1 would have expected that if I had any dream, it would center around the things that I was preoccupied with but this was not the case. And this was what kept me wondering. From the divine to the bizarre, I never knew I was in a spiritual warfare. I was wasting my time focusing on the mundane. These were not some kind of hollywood series. They were real. They were revelational dreams, dreams that showed pockets about my future, my destiny, my purpose, my life. He had expected me to do something – pray, wait on Him, praise Him, worship Him! I did not do it. I was running around asking questions and looking for interpreters, handling the issues of my life carelessly with people who had no business with me. The more I shared my dreams, the more vicious the attacks. He had given me the answers. They were in my prayers and in the word of God. He had given me some glimpses into things that were happening around me and some hope of a great future but I was not sensitive. For the purpose of this book, I will share a few of the things God enabled me to pick from the realm of the spirit. Some are so sensitive, I don't have the words to describe them and so may not be able to articulate them in this book. Like Joseph in the Bible, I may have been the last person to understand their significance. By the time I stopped subjecting my dreams to public interpretation, a lot of damage had been done in my life.

> *For God speaketh once, yea twice, yet man perceiveth it not. In a dream, in a vision of the night when deep sleep falleth upon men, in slumbering upon the bed; then He openeth the ears of men, and sealeth their instruction, That he may withdraw man from his purpose, and hide pride from man. (Job 33:14-17)*

That God chose to manifest Himself to me again and again through His son, Pastor Enoch Adeboye even when I was not a member of the Redeemed Christian Church of God, shows the depth of His love for me. He showed me so much mercy. My journey would take me years of pain and tears, rejection, loneliness, demonic invasion and infiltration, tragedy and finally of triumph in Christ Jesus. I must say I remained in a state of infancy for a very long time because I was not ready to let go and let God take over. So, spiritual matters were not clear to me. My challenges were deeply rooted in the spiritual and I was dealing with things in the physical. God was revealing and showing me things in the midst of so much noise around me. I was going for deliverance and counseling services while I sank deeper in despair.

In the Open Heavens (a daily devotional) of the Redeemed Christian Church of God, authored by the General Overseer, Pastor E.A Adeboye, **Volume 9, 2009, Friday June 5**, titled **HANDLING DREAMS**, it reads:

"Dreams can be a very strong motivating force that can see you through the difficulties of life. Never give up on your dreams. Had God shown you or promised you that it shall be well with you, believe it and stick with it because it shall surely come to pass. "for the vision is yet for an appointed time but at the end, it shall speak and not lie: though it tarry, wait for it; because it will surely come, it will not tarry (Habakkuk 2:3). Your dream will surely speak, that is, it shall materialize. But always remember God has an appointed time for the dream to manifest.... One thing God is interested in which will also determine the outcome of a dream in your life is how you respond to dreams...... Get committed".

Similarly, in the same devotional of Friday May 29, 2009 titled **DREAM: A MOTIVATOR,** Pastor E.A Adeboye wrote the following;

"There are basic reasons for dreams. There are secondary dreams which are given to others which are meant to help you. However, there is an ultimate purpose for dreams. It is to keep you going especially in hard times when everything looks bleak and you are not sure of what may happen. If you have a dream that you look forward to, it will prevent you from giving up or even committing suicide in the face of hardship. There are some revelational dreams or childhood dreams that may not be fulfilled in the next 10, 20, 30 or more years. It doesn't matter. As long as you are sure it is from the Lord, hold on to it.

It shall connect with other dreams and eventually materialize. In this sense, dreams are very powerful . Any dream God has given for your life is worth dying for. Never let it slip through your finger". "If you look at the life of Joseph, you will realize that he was greatly motivated by his childhood dream. And he stuck to it throughout his travails until it came to pass. Never allow anything or anyone to separate you from your Heaven-sent dream. Once you give up the dream of your life, you may have nothing else to live for. When Joseph was thrown into a pit in Genesis 37:23-24, he knew he would not die. If he died, how would his dream of his brothers bowing to him be fulfilled? When he was sold into slavery far away from his place of birth, he knew his dream will come to pass. In Genesis 40:14-15, when Joseph asked the butler to remember him, he was actually saying he knew he was not going to die in prison because his dream had spoken good concerning his future. If there was one person who stuck to his dream, it was Joseph.

Another person who held unto his dream was Paul. In Acts 23:11, the Lord told him he would testify of Him in Rome. He went through several problems and formidable hindrances yet, he held on fast to what the Lord had told him. He knew when they suffered a shipwreck and everyone's life was in danger that he would outlive it. Has God made you a promise? Has God given you a dream? Hold fast to it. It shall come to pass. You will not die before the realization of your dream. Hence like Joseph, cut off everything that can separate you from the One who will fulfill that dream".

> *And the book is delivered to him that is not learned, saying, read this I pray thee: and he said, I am not learned. Wherefore the lord said, forasmuch as this people draw near me with their mouth, and with their lips do honor me but have removed their hearts from me, and their fear towards me is taught by the precepts of men: therefore, behold, I will proceed to do a marvelous work among this people, even a marvelous work and wonder: for the wisdom of their wise men shall perish, and understanding of their prudent men shall be hid. (Isaiah 29:12-14)*

I had no personal revelation of the word of God. I didn't understand the Prophetic Books also; in fact I hardly opened these books. Owing to this deficiency, most of what I gleaned in the spirit looked very strange and no one could give me accurate interpretations. I bought books about dreams, and some of these books touched on psychology and the astral world, things I didn't quite understand, though a few proved useful.

> *And they said unto him, we have dreamed a dream, and there is no interpreter of it. And Joseph said unto them: do not interpretations belong to God? Tell me them I pray you.*
> *(Genesis 40:8)*

I might not have had the interpretation of my various dreams; however, I never wished them away or forgot them. It wasn't the marriage, it wasn't the tears I was shedding, and it wasn't the betrayal, rejection or opposition, no, no, no! Those were shadows. It was my destiny. It was my life. I would go through things, strange situations were common place, I didn't understand. But I had an anchor and I had a hope, in Christ. My dreams were God's revelations and they were sensitive. Some of the experiences are hard to describe. On the other hand, the enemy waged a relentless war. The assaults were overwhelming especially as I had not yet developed spiritual muscles. I faced the most bizarre in the demonic world. That I am alive to share these experiences has nothing to do with me but the grace of God that saw me through it all. He had chosen to glorify His name in my life even before I was born and He could not let me die in spite of my near-death experiences.

God is indeed faithful. That I recorded defeats in my battles showed the extent of my spiritual lethargy. Below are some of the dreams I am inclined to share and they are recorded exactly as they came. A few others are in some later chapters, but the ones shared are just contextual and illustrative.

DREAM ONE. (MARCH 9, 1996) THE ANOINTING

I am in The Redeemed Evangelical Mission and the auditorium is full. The guest Minister, Pastor Enoch Adeboye is in attendance. His preaching is very solemn. He finishes and announces that he wants to anoint members of the church. While he is on the altar, there are quite a number of body guards, dressed in sky blue shirt and navy blue trousers. I am sitting on the right hand side of the church and he starts the anointing from the front row. He instructs that people should place their hands on his face and thereafter on their own faces. His face is radiating and glowing, it is so brightly transparent as if covered by some extremely bright oil, like a neon colour (I cannot really describe it, I have not seen anything like that before). Before I knew what was happening, the man of God is at my side. I am sitting on a long bench with about eight to ten other people and I am the second person on the row. A woman is before me. The woman before me cannot look at his face and cannot touch him. Anytime, she attempts to look at his face, she cannot but she manifests and wriggles like a snake and it looks like she is about to die. Pastor Adeboye does not even look at her. His eyes are fixed on me intently and I am looking at him but cannot touch him because of the woman. And he stands. Suddenly, the whole church erupts in anger over the delay and people shout at me to push the woman out of the way so that Pastor Adeboye can attend to me and go on with others. I muster all the strength in me and push the woman, and she falls flat on her face and as soon as I do this, the man of God steps right in my front. I put my hand on his face and "plaster" my face immediately as he instructed. As soon as this is done, the man of God turns away quietly and as he leaves in a long convoy of vehicles, I woke up. At the time I had this dream, I was not yet a member of The Redeemed Christian Church of God.

DREAM TWO. (OCTOBER 19, 1996. Saturday afternoon) HE NEEDED ME (NOT MY CAR)

I am in The Redeemed Evangelical Mission for a programe. Pastor Enoch Adeboye is the guest minister and I rush from the rear of the church to the seat opposite him. I discover that the notebook I have is full, so I rush back to pick another one and return to take down sermon notes. After the preaching, I get to know there is no car to carry him back. So they decide to use my car. A driver is assigned to him and he enters and sits at the back without uttering a word to either me or the driver. I sit in front with the driver. As we are approaching my house, I feel like asking him to pray for me but I hesitate knowing that surrendering my car to him, I had already received enough blessings, so I don't. I thereafter lift up my hands in anticipation of the blessings

I felt I had received. So my hands are up until the car drives into my compound. He has not spoken a word to anyone. I decide to go back with them so that I could pick up my car after my things had been dropped in the house... (I cannot remember the dream beyond this point). I had also noticed that in that dream, my house was bigger than usual with underground water facilities, pipes and water tanks.

I woke up to find my two hands in an upraised position. As I was meditating on that dream, I concluded that the Lord had need for the car and I would give it.

Few weeks later, even as the dream was burning in my heart, our church had invited a guest Minister for the midweek service. The Minister had asked that we challenge God and give to Him something that would cost us and I thought this was the confirmation I needed. Readily, I felt that was the dream that God had given to me. Without further hesitation and discussion with anyone, I dropped my car in the church and I felt some peace afterwards. My son was just a little over two years old at the time.

DREAM THREE. (MARCH 27, 1997. 11.17pm) THE SEIGE IS OVER

In my village, on a piece of land some distance away from my father's house, is my father's land; (in real life, it is my mother's garden, but in the dream there is a storeyed building on the land). The dream is in this setting. This building is inside a thick and muddy river. My father, mother, elder sister and I are upstairs. Pastor Enoch Adeboye comes out from one of the rooms. We had all lined up when he came out. He has been fasting for the past five days, I am also fasting. One member of the family wants to offer him food, I protest that he will not eat so no such attempt should be made. We are standing in one room while he is in another room praying before he comes out to meet us. As we are there, the whole atmosphere changes. It is dark, thick darkness, boisterous, windy, thunderous, heavy flashes of thunder; as well as a surrounding air of foreboding. Soon, the man of God comes out, and beckons on somebody (not any of us) probably, his aide and tells him : "Tell them the siege is over" The aide turns to us and delivers the message : "THE SEIGE IS OVER". Pastor Adeboye goes back in and shuts the door. I start dancing and saying "O, the siege is over, the siege is over" over and over again. Everything about the dream now centers on me. I start descending the staircase to get back to my father's house and I enter the river. The river is dirty and muddy but the current is very fast. I am swimming and struggling with the current. The river has stretched far. I am swimming the distance and I get to where the river stops, right in front of my father's house, and as soon as I step out, there is a clear demarcation between the river and the frontage of my father's house. The sand is pure white and dry and the sun is shining and the atmosphere is very bright. I step out to this dry ground and immediately, I woke.

At the time of this dream, I was not able to discern much spiritually. I talked about it and I was happy with the dream. But I never took up the dream in prayers nor asked God for interpretation. Even if God did however, I was too consumed with having the marriage back than to bother about any siege. "Was there any siege"? I reasoned? And so anything or any appearance outside the context of the marriage; I viewed as a distraction. But nothing was happening in that direction. I was in complete lockdown. I took the dream literally, that's why I was happy when I woke up. But, I didn't know that the message in the dream was deeper and heavier than I thought. I did not realize that the storms were gathering and would be greater than the marital discomfort and that it would only take the mercy of God to pull me through.

DREAM FOUR. JANUARY 27, 1999. THE WOMAN AND THE DRAGON

My son who was just over four years old and I are sleeping in my bedroom. Then God opens my eyes and I see the ceiling of my bedroom open with some frightening and morbid sound. Some wild, panting, violent and large monster, a dragon-like snake that fills the end of the ceiling to the other. It is baring and spreading its fangs, opening and casting out of its mouth water as a flood. The sound of the water is exactly like that of a surging ocean. (This is hard for me to describe). I freeze. The monster is spreading its fangs and coming towards my son and me. The sight is more than eyes can behold and I am transfixed. In the midst of this wild and satanic drama, with so much struggle and fright, I manage to drag my son and open the door into the sitting room to escape the invading demon. After this dream, life became extremely difficult for me but I held on to Jesus even though I was still not mature.

DREAM FIVE. (FEBRUARY 1, 1999) THE THREE SEEDS

I dream that there is a special Holy Ghost service at the Redemption Camp in Lagos. The camp has an unusually large crowd, an unprecedented multitude. It looks as if the crowd extends to all the neighbouring states like Oyo and Ogun States and beyond. The General Overseer, Pastor Enoch Adeboye is ministering. After the ministration, he announces that God has given him three gifts for three people. These gifts are **THREE SEEDS**. At this juncture, the camp explodes. When he made this announcement, there was complete silence despite the multitude. No sound was heard. And people started pressing forward from the neighbouring states to the front of the altar. It was a wonder. Despite the announcement and the struggle by everybody to make their way to the altar, there is no stampede. There is not a single space left in the camp. Everywhere is full. Even people that are trying to come to the main camp do not have space to walk or run. And immediately, the atmosphere changes. It becomes gloriously cloudy and very solemn and a bit cold (I cannot describe the weather but it was wonderful). Then, the man of God makes further announcement. He gives conditions/instructions to the three people who would be blessed to pick any of the seeds. And the moment finally arrives and everywhere is dead silent. Everybody is anxiously praying silently and waiting. Pastor Adeboye throws the seeds into the crowd and the multitude erupts. THREE SEEDS! I am blessed. I got one! So many people around me struggle fiercely to take it from me, but they cannot succeed. As soon as this SEED is secure in my hand, it explodes and grows rapidly and assumes the size of a mountain. The whole multitude turns to me to beg to pluck it. And I am still giving. I have given out so much and it starts diminishing and it is not growing again so I stop and I tell myself that I am not giving again because it has gotten too small. Hundreds are still pushing to come to me and I turn around and resolve not to give to anyone again. As soon as I stop and turn around, Pastor Adeboye is right there by my side shocked at my complete disregard for the instructions he had earlier given concerning the SEEDS. He looks at me with pity and displeasure at my action. I am holding on to what is left tightly in my hands still surrounded by this multitude but I have resolved not to give any longer and I have not. As the man of God is still there, looking at me, with the seed in my hand, I awoke.

DREAM SIX – (NOV. 23, 2007). HIS DEATH WAS NOT IN VAIN..

Precisely on this date in a night dream, I was given two purple mini-books authored by the late Kenneth E. Hagin titled "**HIS DEATH WAS NOT IN VAIN**" I was asked to read the contents. "**HIS DEATH WAS NOT IN VAIN**", I kept thinking and meditating upon the phrase when I woke up. God was speaking.

DREAM SEVEN. (FRIDAY JULY 10, 2009. 6.25am) WOMAN, THOU ART LOOSED.

I had already woken up from sleep as early as 5.45 am and I am lying down and I am meditating. Then I slip into some light trance-like sleep. I see a very prominent figure in the country (a lawyer) accompanied by a gentleman named Chris. They are walking towards me and a conversation ensues. "I know you" says the Lawyer. He tries to hug me and strike a conversation but it is difficult for me to open my mouth. Although he is not getting any distinct response from me, he is however not in a hurry to leave. Chris is standing by him smiling. As I am struggling to speak to them, I discover that my whole face and head is tightly bandaged except with two-razor slit holes for my eyes. The man puts his finger through one of the slits as he wants to see my face and hear what I am saying. Suddenly, the tight cloth snaps and starts dropping and instantly I open my eyes. As soon as I open my eyes, I literally feel a "lifting" off my face and I am shocked.

> *Unto thee it was shewed, that thou mightest know that the Lord he is God; there is none else beside him . (DEUT 4 :35)*

At this time, I could only mutter prayers of convenience. I was not speaking to things then as I should have done. I had not fully understood the tremendous power in the name of Jesus and the power in the precious blood of Jesus. So I was mouthing the name and the blood of Jesus mentally. I did not know how to study the Word and meditate upon it talk less of applying it to my situation. Some of these experiences were repeated over and over. I did not open up my spirit, I was busy praying my will. It would take me years to fully understand my life

CHAPTER 9

THE SIEGE

As a little girl, I had my dream. Dream of being an international singer, a writer, with a happy family travelling all over the world and having fun in whatever ways I could. Sadly however, I had never given God a place in any of these plans. It was just the pure fantasy of a little innocent girl. We all do have plans and dreams. But, sometimes the dreams are insignificant compared to the higher and better plans that God has for us. He does always have a better plan because He is the Master Planner.

When God delivered the children of Israel from Egypt miraculously, He gave them a command to obey and serve Him only. He warned them that if they disobeyed Him, they would face the consequences of their disobedience, one of which would be a siege. He entered into a covenant with them. When they obeyed God and lived holy, they enjoyed the full protection, increase and favor of God as benefits of the covenant. But when they disobeyed God as they did so often, they suffered dearly for their disobedience. Most times or almost all the time, they were in bondage and captivity as the consequence.

> *And he shall besiege thee in all thy gates, until thy high and fenced walls come down, wherein thou trustedst throughout all the land; and he shall besiege thee in all thy gates throughout all thy lands, which the Lord thy God hath given thee. (Deuteronomy28:52)*

When there is a siege, there are casualties. There is helplessness and hopelessness and the victims are under severe attack. And there are reasons for a siege. A siege is a desperate situation. It is a time where the king, ruler, head of the family or anybody cannot render any help. And it is only from one source that help comes from – God! I was under a spiritual siege, a situation that affected all other realms in my life which I was ignorant of.

> *And it came to pass after this, that Benhadad king of Syria gathered all his host and went up, and besieged Samaria. And there was a great famine in Samaria; and, behold they besieged it, until an ass's head was sold for fourscore pieces of silver, and the fourth part of a cab of doves's dung for five pieces of silver. And as the king of Israel was passing by upon the wall, there cried a woman unto him saying, Help, my lord, O king. And he said, if the Lord do not help thee, whence shall I help thee? Out of the barnfloor, or out of the winepress? And the king said unto her, What aileth thee? And she answered, This woman said unto me, Give thy son, that we may eat him today, and we will eat my son tomorrow. So we boiled my son, and did eat him: and I said unto her on the next day, Give thy son that we may eat him: and she hath hid her son. And it came to pass when the king heard the words of the woman, that he rent his clothes; and he passed by upon the wall, and the people looked, and, behold, he had sack-cloth within upon his flesh. (2 Kings 6 : 24 -30)*

The Israelites were under siege because they rejected God's leadership. They were surrounded by the enemy. Those who were inside could not go out and those who were outside could not come in. There was no help. It was so bad that only the rich could afford dove's dung and later women began to eat their children. There was death, famine, poverty, sickness, confusion, affliction and every evil anyone can think of. God allowed them to go through the siege so that they would turn their hearts to God alone. Israel suffered until God intervened and turned their situation around.

I had rejoiced over the message that I had received in the third dream – "THE SIEGE IS OVER" and I felt whatever I was going through was over. I did not even know whether I was in the midst of it or it was just beginning. Looking back now, my prayers were more of complaining and murmuring, not heartfelt authentic prayers. One thing I never did at this time was stop and examine my life, repent wholeheartedly of any misdeeds or sins and handover my life completely to Jesus. Everything pertaining to me came under that satanic siege. Even my son was not spared the dreadful attacks. He and I had harrowing experiences and escaped death on several occasions. If the siege was physical, maybe my persistent cries would have attracted some physical intervention and I would have been rescued. How do you fight forces you don't see? Every gate is locked, friends become foes, the sun refuses to shine and the moon withholds its light.

I had no answers. There were unexplained losses, withdrawn favour, hostilities and formidable oppositions. I had become the given. Those that tried to help demanded homage. All kinds of bondage had cropped up, challenges of inexplicable magnitude. The siege demanded my soul. My world was spinning uncontrollably. Everything I could hold unto slipped out of my hands uncontrollably. I had no idea how to deal with this siege.

My only consolation at that time was that I was working and I had some money to take care of myself and my son, although the stress of the job too was unbearable. Despite my supposedly good job however,

I was still struggling with finances. I had the most formidable attacks ever at this period. I was robbed at gun point on at least three occasions and each time, I lost valuables. Battles were erupting on all fronts and I was trying to fight them my own way, and I employed physical weapons. Each time, I failed. I was battling to make sense of my life. I faced terrible hardships and my young innocent child sadly became a co victim of these battles.

I was in total bondage. I was struggling at everything at this point. I struggled to pay my house rent and other bills, I struggled to keep my son in school, I struggled with my job in the office and I struggled to survive. I thought I was living right but I was not. I thought that if the marriage had worked, all my problems would have been settled. So I continued to talk and pray about it year after year thinking my deliverance and breakthrough would come from the restoration of that marriage. So I held on, choked almost to death. But as long as I had not handed everything over to Jesus, He would stand afar, never interfering with my will. I was struggling to live a life that pleased God; not even knowing His ways.

My ignorance of the Word of God and my redemptive rights in Christ was taking its painful toll on me.

CHAPTER 10

THE "DARKNESS AND BURDEN" OF LIGHT AFFLICTION

For our light affliction which is but for a moment, worketh for us a far more exceeding and eternal weight of glory. While we look not at the things which are seen, for the things which are seen are temporal, but the things which are not seen are eternal. (2 Corinthians 4:16)

I had magnified what should have been extinguished in seconds to the detriment of my joy and spiritual growth. I had given credit to what should not have been credited in the first place. The issue did not deserve such attention. We have all made mistakes at some point. But where the mistake became the focal point in one's life and sapped one's strength, then it was time for self-examination.

The Bible says our "light affliction is but for a moment". Similarly, if a light affliction works an eternal weight of glory, then mine was not an exception. Surely, there was something I didn't know but which the Heavens were trying to communicate to me. How could Apostle Paul call his afflictions "light"? It could only be because he knew the challenges were fleeting. He had suffered great affliction yet he called it light. Shouldn't we do the same? When Jesus was crucified, instead of railing and cursing and being defensive, He forgave his persecutors. He knew the glory would outweigh anything humanity had ever seen or heard. So he suffered joyfully. Apostle Paul knew that God is greater than any affliction, so he chose to see every obstacle as surmountable.

The second point is that our affliction is for a moment. Apostle Paul did not dwell on his sufferings and so they could not make a permanent abode in his life. That was why he made advances for God. Could I say the same thing about myself? I had chosen to ignore the seemingly clear signals and concentrate on issues that were of no eternal value. As long as I did not see the challenges in the right perspective, I would continue to suffer and believe that God required more stringent measures to approach Him before my prayers would be answered. Not because I was not hearing the word of God or that the circumstances around me were not calling for a change, but I blatantly wanted God to work my will, making my response less than perfect. I depended on things on the outside instead of depending on the greater One inside me.

The affliction is not just light and for a moment, it "works for us a far more exceeding and eternal weight of glory". If I had grasped the revelation of this scripture from the onset, I would have been singing praises to God because the outcome was assured. But I kept struggling and fighting so I could not get out of the wilderness. I did not think of the glory, what glory? That would sound like mockery. But His Word never fails. The affliction became a heavy burden; a burden of making explanations, being perceived as a failure, and trying to live up to people's expectations. Consequently, a situation I should have accepted as a light affliction became the elephant in the room. I had allowed the enemy deceive me into thinking that the affliction was permanent and insurmountable. By this time, my attitude in the office was less than perfect. I had been so affected that I lost my enthusiasm. No wonder things were getting worse despite the intensity of some religious practices like fasting.

Far away in the United States of America, the young man, hiding behind the excuse that I called off the marriage had "moved on". When he finally showed up about seven years after his son was born, it was a trip to show his people and his entire community the letters I had written calling off the marriage and insulting him. If his telephone calls and letters did not convince them, then his physical presence achieved the purpose. I became the object of discussion and derision in local and village gatherings and I wondered if God had not forsaken me.

Thy word is a lamp unto my feet, and a light unto my path. (Psalm 119 : 105)

When you walk in darkness, the word excites you and you cannot apply the Word meaningfully to suit your situation. Everything around you is bleak and you end up depending on the wisdom of men. You are in darkness when you go through things in endless cycles and believe and confess that "God's delay is not denial" hoping that one day, it will be better. You allow the one you should lead to lead you and the one you should minister to, ministers to you. Roles switch and you may not even know.

From my childhood, I had always loved to read. After my spiritual birth, I was fascinated by books from renowned men of God such as Rev. Kenneth E. Hagin of blessed memory, and those of his son Rev. Kenneth W. Hagin, Pastor Enoch Adeboye, Bishop David Oyedepo, Pastor William Kumuyi, Bishop T. D. Jakes, Oral Roberts, Max Lucado, Joyce Meyer amongst others. But I did not apply the biblical revelations contained in those books to my life and situation.

The world was celebrating the advent of a new century (Y2K) and serious minded Christians were looking forward to better and greater experiences in the Lord. I was recounting some wrongs I had suffered in a forgotten century. God was however speaking and He did everything to get my attention. I had not forgotten the letter from Pastor Enoch Adeboye. "Listen to the Holy Spirit". My mind and heart were so chaotic that God chose to reveal things to me in ways He knew best; when I had some sanity during my sleeping hours.

Hear, ye deaf; and look ye blind that ye may see. Who is blind but my servant? Or deaf as my messenger that I sent? Who is blind as he that is perfect and blind as the lord's servant? Seeing many things that thou observeth not; opening the ears but he heareth not. (Isaiah 42:18)

I had no reason to be alive because I had experienced so much demonic assaults and they were intense. I could not vouch for the spirits of some once "loving and nice" people I interacted with. I had taken a lot of things for granted and assumed some relationships were normal. All around me was darkness and I thought I was walking in the light.

My son's father returned to Nigeria in 2005 this time to show his family and village people his "American Green Card wife". He had told me that since I called off the marriage, the woman had been begging and pleading to return to him and he had no choice but to accept her. There was no argument. What was not entertaining in this whole drama was that, he had promised to see his child on arrival. My son was very happy and was very expectant. He however wept and became inconsolable on learning that his father had actually arrived Nigeria, visited his village and returned to the United States without seeing him.

He nearly fainted from the trauma and I was distraught as I held him in my arms helpless to stop the torrent of tears.

CHAPTER 11

UNITED IN GRIEF

For my life is spent with grief and my years
with sighing; my strength faileth because of
mine iniquity: and my bones are consumed.
(PSALM 31:10)

My extended family was closely knit except for occasional and spontaneous ignorant skirmishes bordering on the gender of the children and other very insignificant issues that sometimes threatened our peace as a family. One thing my father never did enough was thanking God for that one male child he had. But he constantly wished he had more. His relationship with my brother was not perfect but it was cordial by and large. As a family, we managed to pull through always. An underlying stress was whatever inheritance my father had was in the custody of his brothers because they had numerous male children and my brother demanded the release of my father's properties from my uncles when he came of age. I loved my father, a love not tied to any material consideration and he loved me too.

Back in the university in 1986, I had dreamt of the funeral service of Tete. Disturbed, I travelled home. He had already been buried earlier on that day before I arrived. My father had instructed that I should not be contacted due to the distance. I wish there was one more word I could have said to Tete. I wept.

Apart from the death of my grandparents, I had lost a niece and a nephew who were less than ten years old. I was not too traumatized because they were suffering from sickle-cell anaemia and the possibility of losing them had always hovered in my sub-conscious.

However, the news of the death of my father in 2000 broke me. At the age of seventy-three years, he was still very strong. He didn't lose any tooth, never wore glasses and was not bent over. His hair was just beginning to recede from the center and he would darken his greying hair so he would look younger. My father was very active and he was not one given to health challenges except for his prostate gland enlargement which had been operated on years earlier and the high blood pressure he nursed. On one occasion, he had to travel to the Lagos University Teaching Hospital for an intensive check-up and treatment. My father (a Catholic Knight) had followed me to the Redeemed Christian Church of God and gave his life to Jesus Christ; a very significant step that gladdened my heart. Unknown to me, that would be his last trip to Lagos. I learnt later that when he returned home, he was admitted to a private hospital and was recuperating. He had been heavily sedated and slept for a very long time. Suddenly he woke up very happy and excited. He asked for all of us, calling our names. Within seconds, he dropped his head on the pillow and was gone! What a transition!

The news was broken to me first thing on a Monday morning as I got to the office. My uncle called me and made no pretences about it. I let out a cry that attracted other colleagues in the building and drew sympathy as I wept and wailed. My father! Dead? My father might have been unable to fix my marriage (and nobody could) but he was there for me anyway! As he lay in state, I could not take my gaze off him. Nothing much had changed from his looks. He was motionless, eyes shut as if he was sleeping. The thought of losing my father was unbearable. "Was that it"? I questioned myself quietly. Soon, the coffin was closed forever. And I wondered about life!

If I thought my father's death had devastated me, I was wrong because I wasn't prepared for what was going to show up next. At the funeral service, we sang the popular hymn: IT IS WELL WITH MY SOUL and gathered afterwards for the usual after-funeral family meeting. Everything was said. Words of comfort, encouragement, and the resolve to remain together as a family and we tried to console one another. We forgot to remind ourselves of the uncertainty of life and the need to walk closely with God. So we, his children parted and kept closely in touch.

My parents had four daughters. My immediate younger sister and I were very close. We used to talk like friends. She had married earlier than I and already had a family. Her demise in 2004 reminded me of the 1997 bestselling novel by Colleen McCullough – THORN BIRDS where a family was going through a generational cycle of tragedies. I thought I was finished with tears when my father was buried. Barely four years later, we had cause to gather once again to bid my lovely sister farewell. A professional midwife and nurse, my sister Georgina, was good-natured. Naturally endowed physically, she was the focal point of the family because she was the first to join the medical profession. Every minor ailment in the home was referred to her. Since we were far apart, I would call for expert advice on medical issues.

Three months before her demise, we were together at the funeral of my mother's younger brother (a young man who had a successful career in the banking sector and later retired for private business). Unpleasant things had begun to happen in the family. I could not put my finger on anything but death had crawled into the family and all we could do was weep.

My sister and I had talked over so many things before I returned to Lagos. I thought medicine held the answers to all medical challenges. She had been admitted at a hospital and we spoke the day before she passed on. Her voice was faint on the phone but she called my name distinctly, and I encouraged her to be strong. That night, I couldn't sleep. I saw her in my dream, cold, dead. The following day, there was no response from her phone. She was gone. To her Maker, to give account of her life on earth.

I was beginning to come to terms with grief. I lost my song, I lost my zeal, I lost my enthusiasm and almost lost my will to live. I could cope with anything but THIS! Another mournful gathering! My strength failed me. I had cried so much privately so that I would look strong in public. My loss could never be imagined. I heard the sound of a hearse, (nobody longs to hear it especially if it is conveying the remains of a loved one) and no matter how routine, it reminds the living of our eventual end. The route from the morgue is clear and straight. But the driver decided to pass through the front of our house. I saw the coffin, bearing the remains of my dear sister. Emotions were let loose. A moment I wish I could forget. I wept for my loss, I wept for the pain that refused to go. I wept for the silence that would never be broken. I wept for the secrets, laughter, and the joy we shared that she had taken to the grave. Oh, I wept! With one brother and two sisters left, we clung to each other with tears and with heavy hearts. I started counting, one, two, three, four, one was missing, she had just been laid to rest. Instead of five, we were now four.

There was nothing left to be said!

CHAPTER 12

HE ROCKS MY BOAT

I loved to write, sing, perform on stage and dance. I had a passion for the arts. Even though I had a job, it was not exactly what I wanted to do. My job was demanding and I was sometimes so frustrated that I contemplated leaving. The job however gave me the opportunity to travel to almost all the states of Nigeria making it a bit interesting. All these changed dramatically in 2005 when the bank merged with a smaller bank that took over the management. Although I had picked up some signals, I adopted a wait-and-see attitude. Massive redeployments were carried out and before long, I would be posted out to the real core-banking with some unreasonable and unrealistic financial targets to meet.

> *When thou passeth through the waters, I will be with thee, and through the rivers, they shall not overflow thee; when thou walkest through the fire, thou shalt not be burned; neither shall the flame be kindled upon thee. (Isaiah 43: 2)*

I had reached the breaking point. I felt I couldn't cope any longer. But I kept at it because I needed the money. Long hours of work and terrible traffic to the office and back home, I would normally get in about 11pm or 12 midnight. My son usually stayed up every day waiting for me. He would have slept off or cried while waiting for me to return from work. There were times he appealed that I transferred to a branch near our area or change jobs so I could get home early to be with him. He did not understand. I had no interest whatsoever in this new responsibility but I had to hang in there. In 2006, I relieved the branch manager who had started her annual vacation. I had planned that when she resumed, I would proceed on my vacation and by that time, I would have taken time out to pray and decide whether to quit or continue.

My marketing job had taken me out with a colleague that day. On my return, to my shock, I was given the option of a compulsory resignation or outright termination of appointment by the branch manager who was recalled from leave to perform this duty. It was a massive exercise carried out in the month of November 10, 2006. I had not been able to meet my set revenue target and there was no other reason I could proffer. I resigned. I had no savings, I had no money. I had tried to give my son a good education and so the school fees and the rent for my apartment left me with almost nothing at the end of every month. My heart ached for my son. He was in secondary school and was over twelve years old. I did not understand what was happening anymore. A month or two later, some insignificant terminal benefits would be paid, enabling me to offset some bills and get temporary relief. Being delivered from a job I was enduring, I rushed to my home state Akwa Ibom to explore a potential business venture.

My stay there was equally dramatic. While awaiting a response to my proposal for a business opportunity I was prospecting at the time, I was invited for an interview with a computer manufacturing company that was about to begin "operations". If I was successful, then I would have to settle for the job. I got the information on the eve of the interview and so after church service, a friend offered to take me to the venue. I had jumped into the anticipated "offer" without going first to Jesus. I never took time to wait on Him and ask what next He wanted me to do. I approached things with my own understanding. And I would bear the consequences of my fleshly wisdom.

The venue of this interview was a residential apartment. There was a table with a panel of about three men. Immediately I stepped in, I had an uneasy feeling. Alarm bells went off in my head. Something was not right but I didn't know what it was. However, I sat down and got "interviewed". The job did promise some mouth-watering benefits and the "successful" candidates would meet weekly or as the need arose. I was mandated to be the Secretary. The helmsman of this company purported to be an engineer who once worked with a foremost car manufacturing company in the United States. For the love of his country and his people in particular, he had decided to bring his expertise and experience to help develop his state and provide employment, by establishing this company. For an ordinary man on the street, this was highly commendable and for those of us who were "successful", we were elated and very expectant.

> *With him is strength and wisdom, the deceived and the deceiver are his. (Job 12:16)*

We started meeting at this residence and later graduated to a room in a vacant building. If other people had doubts, they were silent. I took my son from school in Lagos as I had been given assurances that the office would soon be formally opened. We were told that the last hurdle was the release of funds from the State Government. So I was lodged with friends and relations believing that soon, I would move into my own apartment. There were fresh challenges and new experiences. I kept shuttling between Lagos and Akwa Ibom State, attending "meetings", spending my meagre savings on transport and materials to produce the minutes of the "meetings" which always had between eight to ten people in attendance. I was beginning to get very uncomfortable.

> *Woe to the rebellious children, saith the Lord, that take counsel, but not of me; and that cover with a covering, but not of my spirit, that they may add sin to sin; That walk to go down into Egypt and have not asked at my mouth; to strengthen themselves in the strength of*

Pharoah, and trust in the shadow of Egypt.
(Isaiah 30:1-2)

The company had no office, so no chairs and tables. I never got to see any of the directors of the company and none of the technical partners the helmsman talked about. For almost two years, this was what I was doing, shuttling between Lagos and my home state. I woke up one day to discover that the whole arrangement was a hoax and I returned to base.

Nothing had worked, but God was working behind the scene.

CHAPTER 13

WHAT WENT WRONG?

I will sing of the mercies of the Lord for ever; with my mouth will I make known thy faithfulness to all generations. (Psalm 89:1)

In May 2004, I eventually signed up in the church choir because what was buried in me was yearning to be expressed. I had peace and I was happy. But my initial commitment was shaky because of the demands of my bank job at the time. I was not very active but I was always eager to minister with the group whenever given the opportunity. After I left my job, I had the time and I could commit my time to serve God at last.

Singing was not strange to me, from my primary to my secondary school, I sang for fun. As a child, my grandfather always encouraged all of us to sing in the church choir and I continued with this as I entered the secondary school where I also participated in school chorals and seasonal singing competitions. I knew how to compose songs in my little way, and could write too but I did not know the rudiments of music because we were not taught at school. We were only taught how to sing with the different parts. So even though I knew how to sing, I still needed some form of training to be fully equipped for the step I had decided to take. By now, I was remembering how good God had been to me and I decided to get committed and serve Him with the talents and the passion He had so graciously given to me. If I had any intention of singing worldly songs, it was now too late.

But there were issues I had not dealt with. On the nights of December 13, 1996, January 1, 1997, February 27, 1997, December 6, 1997, I had the same dream repeatedly. This was a season I was almost overwhelmed by the multitude of challenges. Singing was the last thing on my mind. Even at that time, I would never have made any attempt to join the church choir because I was completely disengaged and demotivated. But the dreams I had were unrelated to anything I was going through and I was confused. I was in a less conspicuous department and I was content to be there.

From 1996 when I started having these dreams, they never stopped even after I signed up for the choir. Each of the dreams showed me on the altar ministering but always having challenges. I was always chastised or reprimanded. Sometimes, there were complaints about my voice. There was always something that interrupted my ministration and it would always be embarrassing. And since I had no intention of singing then, I did not deal with these dreams. As was customary, joining the choir did not translate to immediate participation in choir ministration as one was required to go through some training for a period of time. But my membership was delayed longer than usual. I did not understand why and when I was finally integrated as a full member, I would still be on the "bench". However, I would participate in the choir rendition of hymns or special songs and occasionally would be called upon as back-up. My challenges had begun. I waited and I grumbled. What I had picked up years earlier were showing up subtly. Maybe I should go to another department, I thought, but my passion would not let me. And I started dealing with this issue in the physical forgetting that the weapons of our warfare are not carnal.

> *For we dare not make ourselves of the number,*
> *or compare ourselves with some that commend*
> *themselves: but they measuring themselves by*
> *themselves, and comparing themselves among*
> *themselves are not wise. (2 Corinthians 10:12)*

One of the values my grandparents bequeathed to me was never to compare myself with others or strive to copy others and this has been my guiding principle in life. While I appreciated and admired the gifts in others however, I have never longed to be like them because God had made me so unique and special and I had not even utilized most of what God had endowed me with. The wisdom of God passes all human comprehension. He has deposited in his children different and diverse gifts and it is up to us to discover what makes us special and different from each other rather than struggle to be like another person. Unfortunately, people spend their lifetime grieving and longing for the gifts and talents of other people. They blame God for not making them like those people and die unfulfilled. When my parents returned, the rules were stricter, although they were quick to compare me with people who were excelling academically. What an irony! If I needed a dress just because I saw it nice on someone, my parents would never buy it for me. That was the kind of background I came from. I knew my strengths and I knew where to draw the line. I also knew I needed some polishing in the art of music and the expression itself. However, I was getting increasingly frustrated. Those that joined after me were ministering very confidently and it looked as if I did not know how to sing. So my complaints sounded as though I was making comparisons, the very thing I hated doing. I only wanted to praise God, not because other people were participating in the praise sessions.

> *Therefore, I will not refrain my mouth; I will speak in the anguish of my spirit; I will complain in the bitterness of my soul. (Job 7:11)*

I approached the leaders finally and requested to take the Praise and Worship session for the midweek service which normally lasts for thirty minutes. Even though they agreed, I sensed some apprehension. But I was given the go-ahead nevertheless. I was beginning to lose confidence in what I thought I could do effortlessly well. They had all the while believed that I couldn't do it. Would I prove them right?

In the body of Christ generally, if one is sensitive to the Holy Spirit, one would easily discern a mechanical praise and the one coming from a heart of reverence to God. We have many good singers but not true worshippers. Too many times, performance and entertainment are mistaken for Praise and Worship. It becomes mere theatrics. Also, so much emphasis is placed on a beautiful voice, a beautiful attire, ability to dance, good diction and state-of-the art instruments. Some take so much pride in their talent and forget the source. God is not against those, but where we place them above a humble and obedient heart and the leading of the Holy Spirit for fresh anointing, then Praise and Worship end up being enjoyed without power and without achieving their purpose. Sometimes, you discover that, a great singer does not spend much time in the Word and in prayers privately but can put up a "highly commendable fleshly display" trying so hard to portray an image that does not exist. It becomes a great performance and appeals to our carnal nature. But God is not deceived. Praise that comes out of a heart of gratitude focuses on and pleases God.

Good music is one of the major attractions in any Bible believing church. It even attracts the unsaved. A good Praise and Worship session where the Holy Spirit is involved opens the heavens, and miraculous manifestations are common place and people leave the service fulfilled. The preacher would also not have to struggle under such an atmosphere. But do we have these experiences at all times in the present-day church of our Lord Jesus Christ?

God is perfect and He is a God of order. As such, I believe things should be done perfectly and excellently. Adequate preparations, rehearsals and intense prayers should be in place before anyone ventures into any act of service for God. Unfortunately, human beings have taken the attention off God, and placed it on themselves. And we end up performing for the applause of men.

Prior to the midweek service, the atmosphere between the leaders and I was not cordial because I had complained. It was under this atmosphere that I had gone ahead to lead the Praise and Worship session. I had no point to prove to anyone than to sing to my God. I went ahead to pick my songs, prayed and rehearsed every day before the service.

> *Be not deceived; God is not mocked; for whatsoever a man soweth, that shall he also reap. Galatians 7: 6*

April 2010. I stepped on to the altar and from the first song to the last, I faltered. I struggled on all the songs I had rehearsed and thought I had mastered, I forgot the lyrics of such simple songs. The back-up singers and I were on different wave-lengths and I managed to wobble to the end. Some people laughed, some empathized while others were outright angry.

I went back home, fell down on my face and asked God "Why? Why? What went wrong? As if it was God that was the cause. Was I trying to please men? Why?" I was so desperate for answers. But I was just wasting time praying because I had been shown clearly what was going to happen, but since I thought I knew the songs, I thought I would pull through. I had become very insensitive to the Holy Spirit. So I left and changed church and decided to quietly attend a new church as an ordinary member. I had stopped going to The Redeemed Christian Church of God. My leaders did not even know about it, but they noticed I was absent from choir rehearsals and services.

On a visit with a friend to a pastor in one of the parishes of the Redeemed Christian Church of God, without discussing anything with the pastor pertaining to this incident (I never knew him before) he looked at me and said " Sister, do you sing in church?" I hesitated in my response. Before I could let the question sink, he said again; "God says you should go back and sing for Him". He repeated the instructions. I started wailing. I said "Tell God, I will sing for Him, in the church that I am". The Pastor was startled. He prayed and repeated the message. And he asked me again if I sing to which I responded. I left.

Why was I crying? I did not want to go back to my church. But by this time, I was getting better spiritually, I wasn't as stressed and irritable as before. I was praising God in the confines of my room. I had seen the areas in my life I needed to work on. My attitude had been wrong, and there was a lot of junk in my heart. I could not have been in disagreement with the choir leadership and had a smooth ride with praising Him as if everything was alright.

Surely, God cannot be mocked. Moreover, the Holy Spirit took me back to the dreams I had over the years concerning my music ministry. And instantly, I realized that the enemy had been in the camp long before I knew it. I humbled myself and discovered that what I actually wanted to do was sing, and God is not interested in empty sounds but He wanted me to praise and worship Him. And God started teaching me how to praise Him with understanding and worship Him alone in the comfort of my bedroom. He started teaching me how to worship Him from my heart and from my soul. He taught me I could worship Him with my lifestyle and with my resources; that I could worship Him with my tears and in my silence. He showed me that I could sing and master all the songs on earth and make all the noise without necessarily touching His heart. Surely, there was more to the praise of God and worship than the physical show of talents and skills.

The enemy came with all manner of provocation but I maintained silence. Thereafter, I had a repeated nudging inside of me to begin to intercede for the group. So I repented and began to make adjustments in my heart. I was determined to love so I made a conscious effort to let go of anything that bothered my heart concerning this particular issue. It would not matter anymore if I did not back-up, that is if I returned. God was definitely taking me somewhere. I had no animosity in my heart towards anyone. Gradually, my spirit became very free, fresh and liberated. But I still didn't return to my church.

***And Samuel said, Hath the Lord as great
delight in burnt offerings and sacrifices, as in
obeying the voice of the Lord? Behold, to obey***

*is better than sacrifice and to hearken than the
fat of rams.*

(1 Samuel 15:22)

When my song and poetry books were dumped by my aunt in the pit toilet, I did not know it would be a pointer to what was to come later in my life. The enemy knew that one day, I will tell the world in songs the great deliverances God had so graciously performed in my life and the unsaved will come to the saving knowledge of our Lord and Saviour Jesus Christ. I knew what God had put in my heart. I surrendered to God and did not bother about anything anymore. The dreams intensified. I held on to Him. I would use what He gave to me to give Him praise. I would confront and conquer what was threatening to shut me up. And I knew without a shadow of doubt that if I did not pursue my passion, I would die unhappy and unfulfilled. After a few years, I hired a young professional to teach me the basics of music.

God had spoken but I had not returned to church. Weeks were rolling by. I woke up one day to find alarming symptoms of an inexplicable illness. I rushed back to my church, to the choir department. To the glory of God, the symptoms I feared so much disappeared completely right there in church.

CHAPTER 14

THE CURSE OF OBSERVING LYING VANITIES

And when he was demanded of the Pharisees, when the kingdom of God should come, he answered them and said, The kingdom of God cometh not with observation: Neither shall they say, Lo here! or, lo there! for, behold, the kingdom of God is within you. (Luke 17: 20–21)

A lot of things had gone wrong in my life. The power to overcome lay inside of me but my concentration must have largely been fixed on the things that were happening on the outside. Some people claimed to have the answers and came with miserable counsel. And I became an expert in doing my own things. The more I applied carnal knowledge to situations, the greater the fall. After so many years of not making progress, I grew weary. I had hit rock bottom and I was losing ground on all fronts. Like the woman with the issue of blood, I was drained physically, spiritually and financially. I got tired of telling the same story, making explanations, and tired of fasting! I felt I needed "stronger prayers", so I started seeking more prayers to get out of the situation in which I found myself. I came to know some "prayer warriors" They are everywhere. There are many spiritual charlatans, who pose as "Angels of Light" to deceive unsuspecting and gullible Christians.

My parents knew next to nothing about spiritual matters. The first experience I had in going after "prayer machines" was immediately after the breakdown of my marriage. An aunt of mine had been "concerned" and offered to take me to a man who she said used to pray and had spiritual powers. My mum and my late sister had objected but eventually, we still went to him. When we got to the man's house, even though I had no spiritual understanding then, I felt very uncomfortable. The atmosphere did not have a holy aura and the "prayer man" who wore a long beard came out with an "attire of many colours". Was I scared? Yes. But I greeted him nevertheless. My aunt went in with him and later emerged. I never heard him pray, he asked me no questions but he only instructed my aunt to tell me to bring a meager amount of money and we left. I was the one that drove and on our way back home, I had a car accident that could have been fatal if not for God's intervention. I could hardly sleep throughout the night as my room was unusually heavy. The "prayer man's" image was a great torment. But I never went back. Having overcome the strange feeling, I completely forgot about it until years later when I gave my life to Christ. As I started gaining spiritual insight many years later, I knew the man was an embodiment of demonic powers.

I could reach those conclusions fairly easily about that man because of the way he looked and how I felt afterwards. But now that I was born again, there were other referrals. "Oh, this man of God, Oh, this woman of God". "They are good and gifted". When such referrals came from a pentecostal, I was easily persuaded because I needed a solution to the lingering problems and I have twice or thrice taken a walk down those corridors. I later came to realize that it is a great insult to God to seek help from the arms of flesh no matter the packaging. That amounts to doubting God, and anything added or subtracted from the worship of the true and merciful God attracts judgement. Jesus, in His Sovereignty had already given me glimpses of what was coming and the eventual victory. That should have made me sit down only with His Word. My case had already been settled. I should only have steadfastly waited on Him prayerfully. Instead, I was looking for instant solutions and physical manifestations.

Such seeming shortcuts were paths to evil experiences. Often, they are laced with satanic maneuvers, magical applications, unholy vessels, instruments of witchcraft and secret societies, appearing like genuine men and women of God. I had given money on some occasions to be prayed for because they demanded for it. Not surprisingly, my situation always got worse.

They that observe lying vanities forsake their own mercy. (Jonah 2 : 8)

They are touted as being very "prayerful and powerful" and so having them pray would automatically open the Heavens. Nothing could be farther from the truth. Even as I was running here and there trying to obtain one form of "miracle" or the other, God was revealing the contents of these vessels, their deceits and manipulations. Unfortunately, despite all the rigour of fleshly exertions in the supposed prayer and fasting for restoration of an old lifestyle, there was no respite. Maybe my case was so "difficult" prompting my quest for deliverance everywhere. But difficult for who? For God?

But they are all together brutish and foolish: the stock is a doctrine of vanities. (Jeremiah 10:8)

The only testimony I had at this time was that the Heavens were shut. Who would dare share God's glory and what was I seeking?

Seeking mercy from the merciless

Seeking freedom from the bond masters

Seeking hope from the hopeless

Seeking the living among the dead

Seeking power from the powerless

Seeking fame from shame

Seeking godliness from godlessness

Seeking promotion from demoters

Seeking light from darkness

Seeking truth from a lie

And seeking God from the altars of evil mortals.

These were evil deceptions. I was postponing my day of divine visitation.

CHAPTER 15

THE PRISON BREAK

Being in a physical prison is no fun. For those who have experienced such, they'll rather have their freedom than be controlled by some laws or someone. In extreme cases, the time for relaxation or other activities are regulated. Sometimes though, one either completes his sentence or they could be a jailbreak (by God or man) or one could get a state pardon. Whatever the case, every inmate wants to be free. If there is a physical prison then there is a spiritual prison too. The spiritual prison however is not seen with the physical eyes but it is more effective and the rules are stricter than the physical prison. Restrictions are applied in most cases although, one could still move around and do things physically.

In a spiritual prison, you are living but dead. You know who you are in Christ Jesus but afraid to declare boldly who you are. You are afraid of the opinion of men, so you would rather wish to be some other person, talk, walk, and act and sometimes pray like the other person. You are in prison when you crave people's approval in what you do and allow their approval /disproval determine your mood.

Meanwhile, your potentials, gifts and talents are deeply buried within you and you are partially afraid of making mistakes or stepping out to fulfill your God given abilities. It becomes worse when you face situations such as mine and allow challenges dictate the way you live your life. Sometimes it is possible that while you are being very cautious of what people will say if you take a step of advancement in your life, you will be shocked to realize that nobody is looking at you and nobody even cares. No wonder someone said, the cemetery is the richest place on earth. There, you will find the best voices unheard, the best writers the world never got the opportunity to read a page of their works, the best scientists, the best preachers, best of all things and yet, they lay six feet in the earth with their talents buried and muted; souls that would have birthed great inventions.

Is it not true that there are some people who have gone to the grave who are afraid to release all God had deposited in them? Is it not also true that people have been so traumatized with the challenges of life that they have allowed issues take over their entire lives until they could not have the will to live anymore? I have seen people who overcame serious adversities, impact the communities and world at large.

Man is expected to love, honor, obey the constituted authority, elders and fellow men and fear God and God alone. It is therefore a grave insult to God to want to jettison your inner convictions and want to be like another person because you want to be accepted by others. I had taken stock of my life, considering all the circumstances that brought me to the point that I was and it was obvious that I was in prison. It didn't matter that I was doing what everybody was doing, there were things locked inside of me that cried for expression and if I dared died in that state, I would have no answer to my creator. If I made mistakes, He would connect me, lift me up and I would keep at it and believe that His love will see me through.

The Lord our God spake unto us in Horeb, saying, Ye have dwelt long enough in this mount: (Deuteronomy 1:6)

I was still circling and comforting myself that all will be well, but how? I was so unbelievably messed up. My life had experienced a catastrophic decline and I kept pushing. I needed a job as the bills were mounting. I was doing any little thing I could lay my hands on so my son and I could be sure of a meal. I had borrowed money and before long I was facing creditors. Anyone that showed me any kind of favour, I took their names on my lips, focused on them and forgot Jesus. My destiny was struggling for survival. It was total chaos but I carried on with a graceful turbulence and a fearful countenance; not knowing what life would hand over next.

December 14, 2009. A friend visited. I had been watching a Christian program by one of my favorite pastors on the television. My friend casually asked if I have ever listened to a daily programe titled **Insights** *for* **Living** on one of the private television stations in Lagos, Nigeria. I had never seen or heard about it, but I decided to give it a try the following day. The instruction of my father in the Lord, Pastor Enoch Adeboye had been ringing in my ears for many years. The following day at 6.30 am I was in front of the television set on this particular channel and the man of God came on. I heard something that sounded like what I had been struggling with. I was spellbound. The message was reminding me of things I needed to know. What a coincidence! I muttered to myself. I decided to keep at it every day. He addressed where I was, where I am and where I am going. Every message preached was on every single aspect of my life which I had been unable to deal with. I was almost crippled, almost looking for strength to even hold on to the crutches. I had seen and heard the truth in everything I was privileged to listen to. I was reassured of the love that God has for me despite the situation in which I was. And it was strange because I thought I had fallen below the grace of God. Then if Jesus still loved me, as I heard, there was more to this whole drama. I became intensely interested in the telecasts. As he preached one day, something rose up in me, it was not a voice, but an inner witness I had suppressed for years. I cannot explain the encounter. My eyes were suddenly illuminated. I had heard these words before but this time, they were different! There were so many things I refused to know. The Word of God held all the answers to my life. I had wasted my time all this while. My deliverance was in my hands. I had allowed every circumstance in my life dictate my space. I needed to have a fresh new beginning. I had gone far too down but I knew with God, a second chance could be counted as the millionth time. It didn't even look as if he was speaking on the television anymore, God had taken over. And at that very hour, I began to mend. It wasn't man's words. Those were words from God Himself, lifting me up. Those were words of power, boldness, authority to rise up and confront whatever had threatened to swallow me up! Powerful words of transformation. I had the power but I did not know it. The words were right in the Bible. God finally had caught my attention. The Holy Spirit was eager to speak if I could only open myself up and study His Word. I brought out my Bible, dusted it, gave my life to Jesus once again and started what will eventually propel me into that which God had destined for me. It would be another journey but this time around, it would be a journey to victory. Nothing changed on the outside, same rumblings but it didn't matter anymore. When God decided to take me on this journey, it would either be Him or nothing else.

And I was in for more surprises. He was more interested in changing me than my circumstances and I readily surrendered. On Wednesday July 21, 2010. 12 noon, this experience was more of a trance-like sleep or vision. In my sitting room, I see two extremely tall men whose heads almost reach the sky. One bears the name of "god of thunder". As they stand, their heads push the sky further up to a point where the sky cannot be seen anymore. Then they return to earth as if saying they want to execute judgment and I start pleading for mercy. And they are asking why I am always asking for mercy and in a split second, the scene fades and I get up confused as to what that meant.

I was scared. It took me quite a while to understand what was going on. Shortly afterwards, I would learn the discipline of God's love "for whom the Lord loveth he chasteneth, and scourgeth every son whom he receiveth."(Hebrews 12:6) There were relationships I needed to have the courage to break and make space for Jesus. There were many other things in my life I needed to walk away from and become more serious if I needed to make a headway in my relationship with God. My life needed cleansing not just from relationships but in other areas.

When I got ready, every power holding me down had no choice than to let go and until you believe God and step out boldly, the prison gates will continue to loom larger and larger. Sometimes the urge to do something is there but we procrastinate and wait for the "right time". The right time unfortunately may never come. I went to God in prayer and made His word my companion. I began to see myself in the word of God and declared what I saw.

Psalm 119:89; For ever, O Lord, thy word is settled in heaven.

Speaking fanciful words or trying to belong to a clique or going places to be seen cannot get you out of this bondage especially where some people have formed some opinion about you. You are not even expected to do things to change their minds or make them change their perception about you and don't be enslaved by the fear of man. Be focused and do that which the father has called you to do and you don't have a point to prove to anyone.

Suddenly but steadily, I began to hear cracks on the wall and darkness gave way to light, weakness gave way for strength and sadness gave way for joy. I was determined that no matter what life had handed over to me, I was yet to manifest the powers and potentials God had deposited in me. I have not yet lived for as long as I breathe, my best was yet to come. I have never compared myself with anyone and it was already late to do it now. I knew who God had created me to be and I would not try to be anybody.

Every day when I woke up in the morning, I declared who I am in Christ. I carried a conscious and deliberate effort to carry this mentality. It might have been a hard work but it paid off and slowly I was penetrating the darkness. Every Christian needs to know that adversity is not just for us to suffer in it and proclaim "its over". If it's over as exclaimed, what lessons have you learnt? If a similar situation shows up or another crisis, can you develop the wisdom to handle it? Or could this probably be a wind whereby you can reach out to other people since you have already been there? Has God used you to birth massive things on the earth by these experiences? Or could it be true that problems or challenges are stepping stones to God's blessings? I had spent many years living for problems, now its time to live for God.

When Moses challenged the children of Israel, he gave them a choice. However, he asked them to choose life for their benefit. He knew if they chose death, they would be damned forever. Every time I come across this passage, my imagination is stretched tight. It's just as if patriarch Moses would be telling me "choose life" and what kind of life if I may ask? Living a good life is great. When God created earth, he gave man dominion over everything.

> *Genesis 1:27-28; So God created Man in his image, in the image of God created he him, male and female created he them. And God blessed them, and God said unto them, Be fruitful, and multiply, and replenish the earth, and subdue it: and have dominion over the fish of the sea, and over the fowl of the air, and over every living thing that moveth upon the earth.*

What a power!! Adam sold out to Satan but God had a better plan of redemption. He brought man back from Satan through the Lord Jesus Christ. Satan became the god of this world. Jesus died and rose and gave us authority over the powers of darkness. Man however will need to believe in the Lord Jesus, accept him, and have abundant life.

> *John 10:10; the thief cometh not, but for to steal, and to kill, and to destroy. I have come that they might have life, and that they might have it more abundantly.*

Sadly, the abundant life has translated into the pursuit of worldly riches, fame and power to the detriment of Christian character. It doesn't matter if King Ahab craves for Naboth's vineyard and Jezebel orchestrates Naboth's death and finally takes over the vineyard. The Gehazi's are still running over general Namaan to collect gifts while the Holy Spirit is revealing to Prophet Elisha.

Does the church still harbor anointed Samsons who have been heavily anointed by God for special projects still go down to Delilah who later betrays and later cuts short their ministry? Is this the life that the bible is talking about? No, it's a life of righteousness for when righteous men battle power and with power, you prevail.

When I began to live, the first revelation I got was that the almighty God has not put my destiny into the hands of any man and I have no right to believe that my success or failure is trance to any man. Yes, God has lined up helpers and lifters along life's path, but they are not the source. Even when all powers from the kingdoms of darkness were arraigned against me, the only remedy was the word and prayer and so I was free to become whoever God has destined me to be.

When I chose to live, I took responsibility for my life and the mistakes I made. I assumed full responsibility and stopped the blame game even if others were responsible for it. I looked at such as misdemeanor and so they no longer had any effect on me. By taking full responsibilities, you are free from people and explanation. I chose life when I forgave myself and what others thought they did to me. You can have the best things in life and still be enslaved by unforgiveness.

Matthew 6:15; But if ye forgive not men their trespasses, neither will your Father forgive your trespasses.

How do you live with the best life offers and still be carrying a baggage of unforgiveness? It is a fact that no one goes through life without being wounded. If you are not betrayed, you'll be stabbed. Cain killed Abel,

Jacob short-changed Esau but they were brothers. Joseph was hated, envied by his brothers and was later sold into slavery. Abraham, the father of faith, the friend of God, had an affair with Hagar (domestic help) and birthed Ishmael and Sarah later drove both out of her matrimonial home. Injustice you would say but life did not cease. Jacob was unfairly treated by Laban, Moses killed an Egyptian, Peninnah provoked Hannah and King Saul plotted David's death severally. Absalom, King David's son, killed his brother Ammon and later attempted coup against his father.

People steal from each other, accuse one another and sometimes falsely too. People's souls and bodies are wounded, hearts broken and families turn asunder. People are being sentenced to long years of imprisonment and sometimes executed for a crime they did not commit and the creator of Heaven and Earth says "Forgive".

Luke 23:34; Then said Jesus, Father, forgive them; for they do. And they parted his raiment, and cast lots.

Forgiveness is a word mentioned by humanity, yet few practice it. People claim they forgive yet, at the slightest provocation reel out offenses suffered from the Abrahamic era. Countries have severed diplomatic relations due to unforgiveness and countless Christians have gone to the grave with the casket of unforgiveness sealed upon their dead souls. In the midst of my adversities were calls for forgiveness. But first I had to forgive myself and take absolute responsibility for my life and what I had run away from. I would learn that forgiving people takes more than mere words. Holding on to unforgiveness was like giving out my entire life to an enemy. It drained me spiritually and physically. It was like equipping my enemy with some sophisticated weapon to attack me further. I didn't think anyone deserved that much attention.

People justify their actions by talking about the broken relationships and the gravity of the offence. Conspiracy, deceit, theft, murders, how do you forgive a drunken truck driver who killed an eighteen year old university student, the only son of his parents? Such grief! How do you forgive a child who leaks the family's secrets that has become so damaging that the society loses the respect the family once had forever? How do you forgive a pastor who is entrusted with souls of the kingdom, turning round to sexually molest the innocent? How do you forgive a rapist who is not satisfied with the act alone but kills the victim afterwards? How do you survive a wicked gossip and slander? How do you forgive a boss who has refused to recommend you for promotions when your colleagues that you were in the same level with have moved ahead of you? How could I forgive my son's father?

I did. Not because I am superhuman or disappointed, it took me long years not because I was so much in love or that my heart was so broken but because I did not know how to. I could confess it and when I had issues, I would be provoked. As I started listening to the word, thanking and praising God in that situation and praying for him and releasing him, I found healing and that situation brought me joy instead of tears.

If you cannot forgive, your faith cannot work and you cannot receive any healing of any kind. There is no micro-wave solution to forgiveness. Unforgiveness soaks up your whole system and appropriate spiritual medication is needed to heal wholly and you do not have a choice than to forgive and forget. You may still remember but you are not remembering with bitterness or tears anymore. It does not make sense living bitter. It is possible that the one who hurt you is not even aware that he did it. If he does knew, he does not care if you are alive or dead and you end up suffering from both ends.

It is good to thank God for those who have hurt us. If Judas did not betray Jesus, Jesus would not have fulfilled his destiny. If Jesus did not die and rise again for our justification, humanity would have been damned.

As long as you are living, you are not exempted from hurts. If you have been hurt once, I cannot guarantee that, that is the last. However, it is not what people do that is the issue but how you respond. These Judases could be the catalyst to your glorious future. You can't insulate or isolate yourself for being hurt. You will never know where the provocation will come from. The relationships you feel very comfortable with today could present a kiss of betrayal tomorrow. Then who do I trust? Trust God! It's only Jesus that will not disappoint. The rest of us are humans.

If you run away from struggles and refuse to confront issues, you may not birth a testimony. The earlier people realize that life will throw up issues, sometimes very painful, so you will overcome it to become what God intended you to be, the better. I chose life. Someone rightly said that intercession is the purest form of prayer. When you intercede for people, you empty yourself of negative feelings. God begins to put burdens on you and as you intercede, you are indirectly praying for yourself.

When I discovered that not everyone that surrounded me had that spiritual connection, I disconnected. Jesus had people in his inner circle. It's not everyone that should have that privilege. Know the identity and the motives of your friends and acquaintances. This is not done by suspecting every little mistake you can guard against unnecessary trauma. Friendship is a priceless gift from God and deeply spiritual.

I chose life. I forgot the past no matter how beautiful or ugly it was and looked excitedly to the future.

Philippians 3:13; Brethren, I count myself to have apprehended; but this one thing I do forgetting those things which are behind, and reaching forth unto those things which are before, I press toward the mark for the prize of the high calling of God in Christ Jesus.

Holding unto the memories of the past losses robs you of the present and denies you of the future. In Christ, one cannot beat his chest that he has attained the highest height. The experiences of the past should push one forward for more exploits in the different realms. No matter how glorious the past is, you can do better. The investment of yester years are still being improved upon today and one cannot use yesterdays anointing for today's battle and no matter how ugly the wants of your past have been like Paul, press forward into a wonderful and glorious future. I chose life. I prayed about everything and didn't talk about everything. I was able to talk about some circumstances that would have like before become disastrous.

I chose a life of righteousness, having the consciousness of the finished work of the cross and of my redemption rights and I chose to walk in that knowledge. I chose life. I chose to speak life. I cut down on all the idle words I was speaking daily. You can talk, and its cheap talk, full of careless jokes, gossips, slander and weak words. When you order your words rightly, your word carries power. I stopped helping God and took my hands out of my life. I allowed him to lead me since I was tired of helping myself because the "help" always became a disaster anyway and when I got tired of trying, I began to live.

I was tired of the draggy life I had lived all my life so whatever I found in the word was what I learnt. Once I decided to live for God, the game changed and the game will change forever.

Friendship however is a gift from God. God never created us to be an island. He made Eve for Adam and also made us have fellowship with Him. We all need someone to talk to and laugh with. So we grow up surrounded by the warmth of family members, friends and colleagues. Sometimes the ties do not remain forever. Parents die, children marry and leave the home and the cycle continues. In this earthly journey, we meet people we like and share our hearts with. We get acquainted with people with similar interest.

It is a wonderful thing to be involved in a wonderful relationship especially if it is with the same gender. Great exploits sometimes come out of a healthy relationship and calamities have also been recorded. We can readily recall the relationship between David and Jonathan, the virgin Mary and Elizabeth. These were great relationships. However, Jesus' betrayal by Judas cannot be forgotten in the scriptures. Ahitophel the wise counselor who gave David sound counsel showed that he was human after all when he took sides against David. After Amnon took the counsel of his friend Jonadab to sleep with his sister Tamar, Jonadab was unfortunately absent when Amnon was brutally murdered. Friends! Friends! Friends!

With the women, it could be fun and exciting. We talk about everything under the sun, we gossip about men and the world's greatest delusion – Love! We talk, we laugh and we cry together. But we forget so soon that this kind of friendship has its seasons. Some leave, some stay, some are destructive, some bridge builders, while some loving and compassionate. Some however are deep and some, shallow. Some stick around when the cloud is dark and unfriendly. There is so much love and energy; at the same time, there could be mistrust, unfaithfulness or deep seated envy or jealousy.

The craze for money, position, power, love, fame and men have torn women apart. The quest for the above has dimmed the powerful instincts God put in the woman to nurture one another. People's secrets have been blown open because a friend spoke up too much too soon and trusted that her confidence is protected forgetting that the other party may have been wearing a mask.

'And one shall say unto him, what are these wounds on thy hands? Then he shall answer, Those with which I was wounded in the house of my friends' Zechariah 13:5 .

Sometimes the betrayal is not all the work of the enemy. When so much attention and dependence have been placed on a fellow human being and man is elevated to the level of a god where God no longer takes centre-stage, the Jealous God stirs the waters and man once again realizes that it is God and God alone that we depend on.

I never stopped listening to the man of God of the telecast services. I bought notebooks and took down every sermon every morning. I was tired of the mediocre and average life I was living. God had done His part. I needed to work out my own salvation. He had put food on the table for me and did not have to fetch cutlery as well to feed me. He had delivered and protected me, and there were things He had equipped me to do for myself. If I did not do them, I would merely exist. I began to understand the Bible and began a closer walk with the Spirit of the Most High God. As I began with the Prophetic Books (which I had never given myself the chance to study since they were a bit difficult for me to understand) I found myself in the Books. I found the answers to long-lingering issues. I was shocked. I saw the dreams and the visions I have had over the years. I saw situations that matched my circumstances. I saw the interpretation to perplexing issues of my life! I could not believe it.

And God began a good work. It was a complete overhaul. I spent time reading the Word, praying and obeying my deepest premonitions. The first task was how to secure and take responsibility for the space God had created for me. I knew that just as every life has a story, mine was not different and I had a lot to learn from my past experiences. I began to pick up the pieces of my life wherever they had fallen and scattered. My recovery was not instant as I was still trying to stand upright. People left and I too left. In some cases, God orchestrated situations that made parting smooth. In 2011, my son got admission to a private university. Some brethren came together and made the initial payment to enable him start school. I blessed God for this miraculous intervention and thanked all those that He used to make it happen. But I knew it was not God's best for me.

My son's education was a major challenge after I lost my job. I had resolved that in spite of the situation in which we found ourselves, he must have a sound education. So I looked for help. Sometimes, when "help" came, I did not go to God before accepting it. Every "favour" was counted as a blessing. I was exerting my strength in everything on the outside to make ends meet. I knew that everybody had their responsibility and it was inconsiderate to expect others to take over my own responsibility. I had received a lot of spiritual truth by now and I had started having an understanding of spiritual matters, so I hid for a while and embarked on a fast to seek the mercy of God and His intervention. I fasted because I did not want to go back and ask others for help and I wanted God to intervene in my finances. Thirty days into the fast, I got two jobs without exertion. One was an office job while the other was a contract job. My son had not completed his first semester when the jobs came, and I learnt some eternal truths. If I had practiced what I learnt from the telecasts, I would not have sought any favour from other people. Any help that came would have been God sending someone to me and not me running after all and sundry. In short, I realized that God was not in my beggarly ventures of that long, difficult period. But I did not and would never forget the genuine Christian kindness of many of the brethren I encountered in those circumstances.

While there are people who help you to get you off their back, there are also those who help because God has given them a heart of compassion. Generally, people give for various reasons and for different motives. Some give and their hearts are not with you. Those with clean motives give without hurting your dignity as a fellow human being. Those are the warm-hearted who feel for you. They feel your suffering and reach out in any way possible to help you. They are not like some that present themselves as friends and helpers but they are secret agents of darkness who give to afflict you and put you in spiritual, physical and emotional bondage. I had learnt so much, and importantly, I learnt that a child of God, must have discernment in seeking or accepting favour from fellow human beings.

Today, I appreciate the few who genuinely had great love and compassion for me. Not just in giving but covering and encouraging me to remain focused that the storm would eventually be over. They remained true even behind my back, interceded and wished me the best. These were the people in whose company I never had to define myself; they desired my company when they would have been minding their businesses. They looked into my eyes without asking questions and saw the desperation and acted. I praise God and thank them.

I could look back now and have a good laugh at my past mistakes. I could also spare a thought about those who thought my life had come to an end. But sometimes as I reflect on the pains of those mistakes, I wonder if I would not have fared better begging openly on the streets than accepting some of those favours. In 2012, six years after I lost my job, I began to live a relatively comfortable and great life.

I had amazing deliverances – deliverances that defied human explanations. I was focused. The demonic dreams and the spiritual attacks had reduced drastically. I now knew what it was to watch and pray. But battles were still raging, only that now, I was no longer running away from them. I faced and confronted my battles directly. I subjected my now drastically shrunk circle of relationships to the Holy Spirit. I was no longer in a hurry to acquire friends and acquaintances. My spirit was getting stronger. I had fresh revelations about life and I was no longer afraid of anything or anybody. I had announced my rebirth, life had started having meaning, and I knew I was on the road to total recovery. I kept listening to the man of God of the telecast services.

Each time I had a new reason to live not only for myself but for my family. The enemy was losing ground in my life, so he turned to my son and I stayed with the Word. I had nowhere else to go to; I knew the truth. Would a dog return to its vomit? I asked myself in low moments which were getting fewer thankfully.

> *To him that overcometh will I grant to sit with*
> *me in my throne, even as I also overcame, and*
> *am set down with my Father in his throne.*
> *(Revelation 3:21)*

One of the greatest truths I learnt to practice which greatly advanced my walk with God was, first of all, to accept and take all adverse situations to God, thanking and worshipping Him. I had come to accept that challenges were part of God's process for rebuilding me and not deadly things that were there to kill me as I earlier thought. Throughout those dark years, I remember complaining, murmuring, crying and talking to whoever cared to listen. So I needed to make some very major adjustments.

For a girl that used to have so much joy, I sometimes had to ask myself if it was actually me that had sunk so low in life.

I released people unconditionally, all who had offended me. And I also gave up dead relationships. With that, my life started breathing in fresh air. And I knew that if I held on to Jesus, and to Him alone, with the fresh revelation I had received, I would overcome the challenges and outlast every opposition. I took time out to laugh at myself and I vowed that no situation in my life will ever keep me bound again. God had broken the gates of brass that held me bound. My prison term was over. I was free.

The trumpet of jubilee had sounded.

CHAPTER 16

THE FIGHT FOR DESTINY

That thou mayest say to the prisoners, Go forth;
to them that are in darkness, Shew yourselves.
They shall feed in the ways, and their pastures
shall be in all high places. (Isaiah 49:9)

I had tried many times to lift up myself but I could not. The enemy was playing some very cruel games in my life but I knew His time was running out. The fact that I had lost so many battles did not mean God had abandoned me; rather I had spoken too many wrong words., words that were filled with doubt and unbelief, words that were based on overwhelming and prevailing circumstance around me. In that kind of environment, no power is released from the inside except defeat and fear. What I needed to do was to keep at the Word and listen carefully to the Holy Spirit. Many children of God have faced so many battles in life. Many have erroneously feared that their problems would shut them down forever. When they get a little respite, they testify and believe that this was deliverance, not knowing that the greater glory is waiting to be unlocked. They allow the enemy's voice to speak louder than theirs. Even the voices of the world ring louder than that of the Christian. Some Christians become so intimidated by their challenges that they almost lose their voices. Such people cannot fulfil God's purpose for their lives.

There were so many accusations against me at that time and I was trying to make peace even with my false accusers. But at that point, it didn't matter anymore. If anyone walked out on me, it was their loss, not mine. However, I guarded my heart. Everything I went through was to shut me down but when the Word of God entered into me, it liberated me. I was determined to shout above the rooftops and drown the voice of the enemy. I wanted to be seen and heard, not for some trivial or worldly approval but as a testimony to the goodness of God. I wanted others to know the awesome power in the Word of God and in His manifold wisdom that had given me beauty for ashes. I wanted the world to know that it is only God that brings life out of a dead situation. I had seen cracks in the enemy's wall of oppression around me. Little by little, the cracks had deepened and widened, giving way to a mighty fall. I needed the inner strength and the discipline to come out of the cage.

When you come out of prison, what do you do? Do you think the enemy will run away from you? The fight gets fiercer and this is where the real contest lies. The only thing the enemy was fighting was to make me blind to the truth so I would judge God unfaithful and also refuse to fight for my rights as a child of God.

> *For there is hope of a tree if it be cut down,*
> *that it will sprout again, and that the tender*
> *branch thereof will not cease. (Job 14 :7)*

I was on a new plane. Regardless of what I was going through, I believed life was not over. I believed I would rise up again. I might have been the one that put myself in the situation, but it did not matter. I held unto my dreams, I held on to the Word of God that He had revealed to me.

Behind me were voices. Voices of accusation, condemnation, voices from the past, voices of cynicism and discouragement. Voices, voices, voices contending with my deliverance and destiny! Skeptics waiting and watching to see the end that many thought would be a final defeat. But they didn't know that I had been delivered, I had regained my focus. I had come to the realization that I had given the enemy too much liberty in my life, to the point that I had almost became a victim of life. The opinion of men had been dictating my steps until I called myself to order, disconnected myself from false standards and began a fight for my own destiny.

While I was in the world, I was focused on the wrong things. The reason I was not bothered anymore was because I was not struggling out of any challenges anymore. I had come to accept every challenge as part of my growth and a window to my destiny. So I was at peace. Now, I had a road map and in order to follow this map and get to my destination successfully, I had to open myself to God and not to man. But God does not dwell in unholy vessels. He would have to purge me. I would allow the great Physician do the surgery so that when I came out, it would be a different me. If I was learning to fight the external, without adequate preparation internally, the internal enemies would swallow up my victories, so I first needed to pay a closer attention to my spiritual inadequacies.

> *Take in the foxes, the little foxes that spoil the vine; for our vines have tender grapes. (Songs of Solomon 2:15)*

These seemingly insignificant and unseen emotions are so enormous and they eventually become strongholds if not dealt with. God so graciously allows us to pass through trials and afflictions, not because He hates us but so that in the process these foxes that are competing with our spiritual lives could be eliminated. A man who climbs Mount Everest must master emotions such as anger and impatience, pride, bitterness, vengeance, malice, unforgiveness, greed, uncontrolled appetite, lust, strife, envy, jealousy that contend with every Christians. Except you overcome these negative emotions, they would stop you from achieving the purpose of God for your life. And even though some claim to have success in their various callings, these foxes may persist as character traits.

I had identified my own emotional shortcomings. They were many but one was pronounced. I had picked up traces of anger from my father on his return from overseas. Also, I was quite impatient, a trait probably stemming from my childhood struggle with a little stutter in speech which made me irritable when other children made fun of me and I was quick to snap. I always wanted everything done perfectly, whether it was ordinary chores like sweeping the ground or making the bed or complex matters like office duties. It is a predisposition that sometimes creates friction with colleagues and juniors who may see one as too fussy. These might be mere excuses however as the enemy had found them useful as fighting gates.

> *Fight the good fight of faith, lay hold on eternal life, where unto thou art also called, and hast professed a good profession before many witnesses (1 Timothy 6:12)*

Throughout the Scriptures, the only fight a Christian is called to fight is the good fight of faith. You cannot be bold to fight for what is not yours. Jesus has already given us the victory and we are to fight from that vantage point of victory. This is a command. It is the bedrock of all other fights. Just as the Bible talks about good success, it also talks about good fight. It therefore means there is bad success and bad fight. Sadly, I was involved in too many bad fights. Fights that had no strategy, direction or preparation. I fought battles that had no eternal value or significant reward forgetting Jesus had already given me the victory. I fought battles that drew me away from my purpose. I fought real and imaginary enemies and I lost. I fought battles that were not mine. I fought those who left and I fought those that stayed. Though I needed to fight, it was not these kinds of fights. The battles were to be done on my knees and with my mouth using the Word of God, making powerful declarations to scatter the trenches the enemy had built around me. The enemy had used every weapon imaginable, including human agents who mastered the art of spiritual manipulation.

I began to break brass in the spirit rather than breaking bone in the flesh. I began to learn to talk less, weighing every word I spoke. More importantly, I gave time to studying the Word and meditating upon it and instantly obeying the Spirit of God. I was unlearning some old beliefs. The one that allowed me to enter this fight had already made a way for me. The enemy was relentless but I remembered the One who died for me and I also remembered that His death was not in vain. That dream was for a time like this.

The fight of Faith is a fight for destiny. It is a fight with the Word of God. You don't fight circumstances. You believe and speak the Word despite contrary circumstances. You "call those things which be not as though they were". (Rom 4:17) It is a fight of love no matter how much you are hurt. Too many times however, some Christians get involved in the wrong fight. They fight one another. They fight for position and recognition in the church. They believe any position of leadership is a position of power. They imitate the world to manipulate situations to favour them. They scheme and control to remain relevant without any spiritual backing. And they forget that Power belongs to God. They strive to be seen by men and not to be heard by God. They believe acquisition of material wealth and other basic comforts of life and trusting in them are pointers to a great destiny. And at the sunset of their lives, they realize sadly that they only spent their lives pursuing what was not written in God's agenda for their lives

> *And the Lord said unto Gideon, The people that are with thee are too many for me to give the Medianites into their hands, lest Israel vaunt themselves against me, saying, Mine own hand hath saved me. (Judges 7:2)*

When a circle of friends is too large, especially at a time one is going through a crisis, God retreats. If He lets trickle down some drops of mercy, it is because of His name which is at stake. When people are too many, you can't hear God and you will unfortunately ascribe His intervention as the work of man. I had learnt very bitter lessons.

Gideon had believed that victory could only happen if he went to war with the multitude but God was not pleased. Even after he had pruned the number to ten thousand, God still had it reduced by putting them through a test. At the end, Gideon was left with only three hundred men, and he went on and got the victory.

When I started gaining strength, I put my relationships under the searchlight of the Holy Spirit. I prayed to God to make me a true friend and also send true friends to me, friends who would share my vision and who would not be intimidated by my success or discouraged by my failure, friends whose heart and energy were pure. I didn't need to be surrounded by a crowd. It is not every friend that is a friend. It is not every friend that knows your struggles that is sympathetic despite the outward show of concern, or even wishes that you be delivered. Some help become a door to bondage and death. People have motives and sometimes very wicked motives. Unfortunately, it was also a period when I saw in their debased state some of the men I had held in the highest esteem. I came to the conclusion that in life, only God is to be trusted.

> *The heart is deceitful above all things,*
> *and desperately wicked: who can know it?*
> *(Jeremiah 17 ; 9)*

Unfortunately, I did not look at heart in my earlier affiliations. I came to realize eventually that life is much deeper and I needed to understand its dynamics and the nature of spiritual things. On the outside, my interaction might have looked perfect but I did not go in the natural anymore. Some of the people might have been good people but it did not matter anymore. My only responsibility is to pray and wish everyone the best at all times. God took me up from eating crumbs to eating at the table He has graciously prepared for me because He is the Provider and the Only Source. Friendship is a covenant but you don't covenant with every friend. God reveals the heart not man. Only by the light of the Holy Spirit were some "sisterly friendships" that seemed excellent on the outside exposed as a dark night of fatally drawn swords. They were terrifying experiences but it led me to acknowledge with even greater conviction that the "Most High ruleth in the kingdom of men." God delivered me from the dangers of misplaced trust and dependence on crumbs.

> *Give not that which is holy unto the dogs,*
> *neither cast ye your pearls before swine, lest*
> *they trample them under their feet, and turn*
> *again and rend you.(Matthew 7:6)*

A closer walk with God calls for total separation. When He asked Abraham to move out, and he went with Lot, the Creator of the Universe knew that His purpose would be frustrated if the two men remained together. The baggage of unprofitable relationships has to be examined in the life of every born-again Christian. The fear of rejection and the desire for affirmation should be resolved with finality.

There were some divine information I took to the market place because of lack of understanding and it was only the mercy of God that pulled me through. There is no crowd when matters of destiny are at stake, no emotional entanglements and spiritual weakness. God "called Abraham alone". Now, when I have information that I do not understand, I look to the word of God.

> *He shall see of the travail of his soul, and*
> *shall be satisfied: by his knowledge shall my*
> *righteous servant justify many: for he shall*
> *bear their iniquities. (Isaiah 53:11)*

I remembered all the sacrifices carried out in my grandparents' home that had not been dealt with even when my parents returned to Nigeria. I remembered the libations and incantations at my traditional marriage. Wicked spirits must have really had a grand feast as no voice was raised to challenge them. Imagine! Wicked powers from the pit of hell that Jesus had conquered and given us authority to trample upon.

It had been years and the enemy had gained sufficient grounds. The effect and devastation had taken its toll. God had revealed so much to me in this area and it was a tough battle but I looked unto Jesus alone. My mother's family was almost desolate. Death and destruction were on the prowl, and the enemy had almost fought me to a standstill. I arose with the blood of Jesus and with the Word of God on my lips. I held on, kept listening to the television broadcasts, kept praying and singing praises to God and diligently studying the Word. I prayed for people and determined to keep my conscience pure towards all men. All the layers of weaknesses were being laid off one after the other. Though the battle was far from over, but now it had become interesting. Behind all the suffering and pain lay an "eternal weight of glory" that no human eye hath seen. Was the marriage restored? No! But had I found a greater and higher purpose? Yes! Would I fight to get back what I lost? I had a higher call. If my "loss" would give room for God to use me in His Kingdom, and He turned the situation for His glory, that would give me closure! I would not fight for the marriage. Not anymore! You fight for what keeps you over and not what takes you under! I had found my purpose, an eternal purpose and I needed the courage and the inner strength to rearrange my navigation.

The pull of God's glory was too powerful to trade for a base and mundane life.

CHAPTER 17

CHANGING OF LORDS

I was back in the arena of life and no longer crying or crawling. I used to cry not because of the marriage but because my son and I were going through a traumatic experience that seemed endless. So each time I opened my mouth, tears would come streaming down my face. I told Jesus to stop the tears as I had cried enough. Then I saw in the Bible where God told me to stop crying.

> *Thus saith the Lord; Refrain thy voice from weeping, and thine eyes from tears: for thy work shall be rewarded, saith the Lord; and they shall come again from the land of the enemy. And there is hope in thine end, saith the Lord, that thy children shall come again to their own border. (Jeremiah 31:16–17)*

Each time I opened to the above Scripture, it was as if Jesus was speaking these words to me. There were some things I could not afford for my son but I kept encouraging him. It did not matter what we ate at home, even if he slept without food, he understood. As I started knowing the truth in the Word of God, I faced my broken marriage and spoke to it.

I can feel the pain of those who have gone through a broken relationship, especially if the relationship was meaningful. It is however not an excuse to mourn a lifetime! I also know how it feels to suffer. Suffering as a consequence of wrong choices, suffering owing to lack of funds to adequately care for yourself, suffering for being ignorant of the Word of God and giving the enemy a foothold over your life.

I clearly admitted my mistakes and also suffered the consequences. But because of the effects of what I was going through and for lack of finances, it looked as if my son's father was still a central figure in my life. No, I had some discomfort especially where the child was involved. The marriage did not enhance me positively in any way, so there was nothing for me to grieve about. However, I give glory to God for the only resultant blessing – a child that I didn't even ask Him for. In spite of the neglect and lies, God had issued a command "Get up or die" or like Bishop T. D. Jakes says "Bounce back or die". I stayed glued to" **Insights** *for* **living**" and the Word of God, I could not but praise God in everything that I was privileged to experience, even the negative ones.

Why do people in my situation cry or grieve? I am sure there is an abundance of reasons. Jesus was now in my boat and I would not proceed unless as directed. My continuous interaction with the Word of God had made me so grateful to God. I believed God's assurances that this situation would work out for my good no matter which side the coin fell. I thanked God for the roles each person played whether it was for or against me. I thanked God for every year that had seemed fruitless and praised Him for my young son. My son and I took out time to deal with his relationship with his father so we could move ahead. The worst was over and we kept expecting the best.

> *Brethren, I count not myself to have apprehended: but this one thing I do, forgetting those things which are behind, and reaching forth unto those things which are before, I press toward the mark for the prize of the high calling of God in Christ Jesus. (Philipians 3:13-14)*

This was one of the greatest steps I needed to take even as I was undergoing a personal development programme. My life had been so affected by what I had been through that I had to make a conscious effort to break away from my past if my future were to be established. My emotional energy had been sapped by issues competing with my purpose. I had to start dealing with those issues. I took my attention away from the people and the things that were constantly reminding me of the past. I had no time to argue anymore with anyone and I gave myself the opportunity to allow new people and new experiences occupy my mind. I began to pay less attention to the voices of the past and I was making steady progress. I began to realize that I was healed when I could talk with ease about my situation and have a good laugh with my close confidants (now I knew them). The things I used to cry about suddenly became what I readily smiled about. I would sometimes wonder aloud what came over me all these years. It was so refreshing and I knew that it was only my knowledge of the Word of God that had made the difference. If I had sat with God all this while, fed myself on His word and allowed the Holy Spirit minister to me, my afflictions would have ended much earlier.

Human beings tend to hold on to their emotional issues. They hardly let them go. What people have done to them take center stage and results in resentment and grudges. Anyone that allows these traits to fester will end up being defined by them and might never be able to overcome their circumstances. The irony here is that the offending party might not even be aware of what is happening.

> *And the Lord said unto Samuel, How long wilt thou mourn for Saul, seeing I have rejected him from reigning over Israel? Fill thine horn with oil, and go, I will send thee to Jesse the Bethlehemite: for I have provided me a king among his sons. (1 Samuel 16:1)*

Isn't it interesting that we hold on to what God has long discarded? Being sensitive to know when its over and moving on with God. But we cling, we mourn, our speeches are filled with what had been on an issue that had long died. It was however time to move on. There was no way I could hold on to the past and expect freshness of life to penetrate my being. Even if we were able to work out things in that marriage, the effects of a faulty foundation would have affected not just us as a couple but also our generations because too many things had gone wrong. And God had intervened because He had a good plan for my life. The work He began in my life was amazing. He was removing all the negative emotions and stripping me of things that would make me needy or dependent on anyone but His Christ. He had to make me whole so that I would not lose my identity in Christ or crave for approval from people who are themselves trying to find their own identity. I had come to love and appreciate myself and appreciate my experiences. And as I began to look up to God as our only source, no matter our circumstances, we were no longer troubled as Jesus was always there for us.

I praised God. He had opened my eyes to see all He had delivered me from. Oh I praised Him. I accepted and told myself it was over, and indeed it was over. I now knew grief must not last a lifetime no matter the loss. Only the loss of God is worth grieving a lifetime.

There were things locked within me I had not yet released. Jesus was calling me for fellowship not mourning. I had attended funerals coordinated by other people. Now, I was coordinating one myself.

At this funeral, only the Father, the Son and the Holy Spirit showed up. No mortal was invited. Funeral rites completed, my son's father had completed his assignment and the dead was laid to rest! I disconnected, spirit, soul and body. A new me, Sylvia, I could smell fresh, clean and holy air.

> *Dearly beloved, avenge not yourselves, but rather give place unto wrath: for it is written, Vengeance is mine; I will repay, saith the Lord.*
> *(Romans 12:19)*

Desiring to avenge has taken a lot of people out of the will of God. Yet, after getting their pound of flesh, many come to realize that it is not worth all the trouble. We easily forget that God is the Righteous Judge of the earth. I had no business consenting to marry a man who was legally married and who had consummated the union. No matter how light the circumstances that brought him together with his wife and no matter how hard he tried to downplay his commitment, there was a subsisting marriage. Probably, he wanted to have the best of two worlds or was simply running away from besetting issues that he himself could not conquer. Whatever his failing, he was only human like the rest of us. We are all sinners for whom our Saviour died on the cross. He too deserved sympathy and forgiveness from the Almighty God. The colour of the card should never have been as issue. Green card, yellow card, black card, or red card; all colours belong to God!

Every day is now worth a living. I am now fully depending on God. I am free as a daughter of the Most High and I can now face life without fear. I have no desire for revenge, no urge to wish him or his family ill. I have come to know that power belongs to God, and I knew He has given me beauty for ashes. But one thing is clear in Heaven and on earth; my son's father has ceased to be the focus of my life.

Lordship has changed. The Merciful wanted me to birth the new.

CHAPTER 18

BREAKING THE CODE OF SINGLE MOTHERHOOD

I tried to play a dual role of parenting but I could never be the man. As I look back, I realized that the strength to be a single mother came only from God. The name "single mother" I had dreaded, had now become a familiar term. I could not run away from it anymore.

Having assimilated so much of God's word, I could not allow myself to fall into more errors in the desire to conform to societal expectations. Some women in my circumstances are tempted to find a male companion that would provide them with some form of respectable cover in the eyes of the public. The pursuit of societal respectability has led many to wrong choices and sinful relationships. Many women have suffered all manner of humiliating conditions; some have been driven to insanity and even death, in the struggle to avoid the tag of single mother. Some have clung to unhealthy relationships that diminish, not enhance their worth. I am not blaming or judging anyone; everyone must live according to their understanding of life and invariably, people have a personal reason for their choices and decisions. For me, I had come to the realization that only what God thought of me mattered. It no longer was of any major consequence what any human being said or thought about me. I had an appointment with God and if it meant that my role in His service was as a single mother, I was content and proud to accept it.

And Abraham rose up early in the morning and took bread, and a bottle of water and and gave it unto Hagar, putting it on her shoulder, and the child, and sent her away: and she departed and wandered in the wilderness of Beer-sheba. And the water was spent in the bottle and she casts the child under one of the shrubs. And she went, and sat her down over against him a good way off, as it were a bow shot: for she said, Let me not see the death of the child. And she sat over against him, and lift up her voice and wept. And God heard the voice of the lad; and the angel of God called to Hagar out of heaven, and said unto her, What aileth thee, Hagar? Fear not; for God hath heard the voice of the lad where he is. Arise, lift up the lad, and hold him in thine hand; for I will make him a great nation. And God opened her eyes, and she saw a well of water; and she went, and filled the bottle with water, and gave the lad drink. (Genesis 21 :14–19)

Hagar, the domestic help-turned mistress (on Sarah's approval) had a child for father Abraham. This was an arrangement made in the flesh by human agents. For Hagar, it was an "assumed" privilege, giving Abraham an heir. But the human scheme was dashed because God had a superior plan.

It is impossible for Hagar to convince anyone that she was minding her business when Abraham came calling. Looking at it from all angles, Abraham's intention was not to disrespect Sarah as she was the mastermind of the whole arrangement. Rather, the couple's desperation to have an heir made them to do the unthinkable. Unfortunately, for Hagar, she did not understand the politics of being a mistress to a man who desperately loved his wife. She thought because she had a male child, she had won the contest. Ishmael compounded her problem and Sarah showed Hagar the way out.

The Bible did not record this but Hagar must have been the subject of malicious gossip in church, market and the entire community. Hagar the "husband snatcher," would be a familiar term used to describe her. Despised by all and friendless, she turned to Abraham, her son's father only to be told that it was all over. If Abraham had any hesitation in sending her away as Sarah ordered, he had to have a rethink because God sided with Sarah. Not because God hated Hagar or Ishmael but because the purpose of God could only be fulfilled in Isaac and for this, there was need for separation. I am sure if Ishmael did not leave with his mother, there would have been some unpleasant consequences for one, some or all of the parties.

But Ishmael is still important to God. Whether it is out of wedlock or a broken relationship, whether it is of outright perverted passion or of a sacrilegious or incestuous union, God gives life. Hagar leaves with Ishmael with "bread and a bottle of water." Abraham bid them farewell with tears in his eyes. He loved them but he loved God more.

On her way, she wept. Hagar wept for so many reasons, but please do not try to enumerate them if you have never been in her shoes. Her tears were much but her greatest fear was for resources to take care of her son. The previous night, Hagar had gone to bed as the "beloved", the next day, Hagar became a single mother, the first since the world began.

Between Hagar's day and today, not much has changed for the single mother. A lot has been written about single parenting. But the world hardly ever gets to hear about single fathers. Why? Because society is kinder to the single father. He is only expected to earn money and provide for his child's upkeep by minders, usually his close relatives. He is even encouraged to take a wife so she can readily assume responsibility for the child(ren).

God created a woman as the nurturer; she is life. No matter what she faces, her primary responsibility is to her child(ren). Her own life centers around them. The bond between a mother and her children is beyond the physical. That is why she can go to the end of the world for their sake. She would rather starve to death than see her children go without food. Even in the midst of a thousand children, she can discern the sound or cry of her own child.

For the purpose of this book, I will only write about the Christian single mother. She is in the same troubled waters as her non-Christian counterpart. But she has the wonderful privilege of having Jesus as her Lord and Saviour. She trusts Him to deliver and save her and knows that He will never fail her. So while the worldly single mother is looking for answers from the world, the Christian single mother puts her faith in Jesus alone.

I actually thought that nothing had prepared me for the kind of challenge; but looking back, I can see that God really did. That I was brought up as a child to wake up very early and exercise self-discipline in anything I did was one of my greatest assets. It worked so well for me. In Lagos, where I operated from two bases several miles apart from each other, i.e. my office and my house, it would have been practically impossible to nurse a child alone. My work schedule involved getting to the office as early as seven in the morning and coming home late at night, sometimes at midnight. Yet, I must be up the following morning to repeat the same rounds. From childhood, I could never sleep for long hours. I grew up not being able to stay in bed for too long like some other women of my age. God had always known what was ahead for me. So for that, I thank God for my grandmother whom He used to prepare me. Life with her had taught me to be resilient and tenacious as I faced tough situations even as a child. When the unexpected role of single parent became my lot in life, the challenge was tough but God had equipped me with the strength to cope very well.

People claim to be experts at knowing others. My experience in life showed me that about ninety percent of people I related with who claimed to know me did not know me at all. To be fair, I too didn't know them. Most of them had no idea where I was going. They saw my struggles and even saw when I was dining with the devil. But they were not there when the game changed. The fact that I ran in a pack at a point in my life did not mean I was a wolf. It only showed that I lacked discernment and understanding at that material time, a stage which by the mercies of Calvary, I have since put far behind me.

A family unit comprises a father, mother and children. Raising a godly and wholesome child requires the active participation of both parents. The cover provided by both parents is necessary for the child's balanced development. But the truth I came to discover is that where one part of that necessary human cover is lacking, the protective power an d wisdom of God manifests in a stronger form if His presence is acknowledged in that home.

I can testify today that I survived because I took a decision that the world would not define my family. I was able to instill faith and understanding in my son that our family is by no means dysfunctional even though his father was not "available". Jesus is my husband and our father.

The role of a father in the life of their children is emphasized in the Holy Bible. Fathers have a responsibility to train up their children and instill in them the knowledge of the Lord. Sadly, there are fathers (even in the Christian fold) who do not take this responsibility seriously and do not impact their children positively. Sometimes, they are not even there for them when the storms of life come calling. Oftentimes, the single mother is left with problems that are multifaceted. The casualty is always the child. Hardly do the feuding parents consider how nasty it is to be fighting over a gift that God gave them to nurture. It is not the heart of a partner that breaks, but that of the child that bleeds. He becomes helpless, confused and left wondering why he is torn between the two most important people in his life, the parents that should have united in love to give him the natural cover. I held my son alone knowing that God was with me. I constantly spoke to him but there were times I got weary. In all, I kept trusting that God was preparing me for something greater than my immediate circumstance. I believed that everything would work out fine since we are committed to walking with Him. I refused to despise myself and my status and I owed no apologies to anyone except to the One that created me.

Interestingly, even from creation, human beings have tended to be mostly defined or identified by their infirmities and failings. Rahab is thought of as the harlot, Cain as the murderer, Mephiboseth the lame, Jabez the cursed, Mary Magdalene the demon possessed, Naomi, the widow, Hagar the single mother, Paul the persecutor, David the adulterous murderer. As soon as Samson is mentioned, the picture that readily comes to mind is Delilah. And Jezebel was so wicked that no one remembers she was royalty; all she is remembered for is her manipulative and greedy acquisitiveness that brought about the death of Naboth. Do these sound familiar?

A kind of stigma is attached to single mothers whether or not their situation arose by choice. The general attitude is shrouded in "mystery" of a kind that speaks louder than words. A divorced or widowed woman prefers to be so called than to be referred to as a "single mother". I would personally advise any young lady to exercise the utmost caution in her relationships and to avoid any situation that might lead her into single motherhood. Some women have found themselves in ugly situations that turned them into the kind of persons they never intended to be, and bearing names that they never bargained for. Life does throw up the unexpected sometimes and the single life may become unavoidable in certain circumstances. An example is when a spouse has died and there are circumstances that prevent a remarriage. Another example is when a woman elects to live alone out of reasonable fear and insecurity that is accasioned by continuous domestic violence, or when there are irreconcilable differences tearing the family apart.

Based on what I have seen of life, I would not readily advocate a separation when chances still exist for remedying an impaired relationship. But clearly, there are marriages that have become mere facades and in some of them, the affected individuals lead lives of pain and extreme misery.

It makes me wonder if the single life with all its connotations of failure and contempt is not a nobler option. I also wonder if society ought not be kinder in its judgment of women living a single life after a failed marriage. Some of these women are strong intelligent women but society is rather too quick to judge and condemn them without caring to understand what they had been through. A woman in that situation must comport herself with more than usual self-discipline and decorum or she would be a subject of more than usual gossip and criticisms. She must also contend with the temptation of getting so preoccupied with her own struggles that she doesn't find room to spend quality time with her children. Children growing up in that situation face their own peculiar emotional challenges. Some become so unruly due to the absence of a father figure in their lives. Some get excessively pampered and spoilt either by a mother that is trying to fill the void or by a conscience-stricken father that is struggling to make up for his absence by sending unnecessary material gifts.

Ishmael was still important to God as we can see in the bible. Isn't it also interesting that the God that supported the separation of Hagar from Abraham is the same God that "heard the voice of the lad where he is" and went on to provide for him.?

Whatever were the circumstances that brought a child into the world, God has an ultimate purpose for that child and the purpose is perfect. Before Hagar and her son left Abraham's house, God had already made all the necessary provisions for the child's upkeep.

So whether the act was deliberate, whatever circumstances a single mother finds herself, God has an ultimate purpose and the purpose is perfect. Before Hagar and her son left Abraham's house, God had already made provision. Some single mothers (including me at that time) become so desperate and employ physical and mental means to deal with situations instead of looking up to God and asking God to open their eyes like He did for Hagar. The result of this blindness leads to unnecessary frustrations and poverty of unspeakable proportion. And the journey becomes longer than necessary.

In our society, it is almost like there are set but unwritten rules for a single mother. There is a yoke of endless scrutiny and non-too-subtle prejudice. Those of them who ignorantly open up their lives to friends of doubtful integrity soon find they have lost control of their lives to others without realizing it. They are the subject of much talk behind their back. People cast inquisitive glances at them and are eager to know the story of their broken life. At a stage, it is as if everyone has a say in your life and anybody could tell you what to eat or wear, where to go and who to talk to. If you laugh loud and seen happy, the ready conclusion is that a "prince charming" has showed up somewhere (and hey, don't they have the right to know?) If you are sad, there is no problem with that because that's really how you ought to carry on because you are a woman without a husband and they want to mourn with you and have something to talk about. They attach reasons to any changes in your life. At a stage, your single status even becomes a yardstick to judge not only your character but your competencies as well.

I have seen and observed things. But the word of God has given me the audacity to break through man-made barriers and announce my freedom. I am no longer interested in some of the things most people are struggling for. I am only interested in getting into the purpose of God for my life. Every other thing has become insignificant. I have promised myself that I will obey authority, live right and respect others. But I draw a line when it comes to my personal life and here, I fear no one but God; I would not entertain anything that would violate my conscience, and I shut my eyes and ears to the opinions of men because I have come to understand a lot more things about the human nature.

And this is the true essence of a woman who knows her worth. If any man desires me, he is not doing me a favour. He is instead honoring himself. He comes, not out of sympathy to carry any weight in addition to his, no! He comes because he has found a priceless jewel who would add more stars to his crown. Unfortunately, most single mothers have missed this truth. Out of loneliness and seeming difficulties, they jump into another marriage that leaves them lonelier and more frustrated, thereby compounding an already bad situation.

I love my son and want to be there for him. By the special grace of God, I have raised him with the type of discipline that my grandparents instilled in me not minding that times have changed. He has grown up to differentiate right from wrong; he knows how to act in every situation and how to relate with people. He knows who to say "yes" to and who to say "no" to. I did my part and I still do but this time, much more of my parenting effort is of prayer because as a young adult, he sees some of my methods, style and manner of discipline as old-fashioned. I accept that indeed, times have changed but experience shows us that the key principles of life are eternal and unchanging. There is no excuse for indiscipline nor would there ever be justification for it. If my son should choose to do anything that is contrary to what he was taught as a child, I would be in my closet on my knees, having a chat about that with God, my Father and his. I have relinquished control of him to his Maker, knowing that I did my part and diligently too.

My parents once offered to keep him while I worked and have some time for myself. I turned this offer down. When he started nursery school and had assignment to deliver the next day; he would wait up for me to no avail because I would always return from work late and leave early the following morning with no time to monitor his academic performance. When I happened to get home a bit early, I would be so tired that I would fall asleep while he was beside me with his writing materials and books, crying and trying to wake me up to help him do his school work. Whenever he was ill and admitted in the hospital, I would stay up watching him especially when he would be drip-fed. When he opened his eyes, he would call me and request that I carry him. He looked so innocent, so vulnerable. It was always a terrible pain to step out and leave him by himself even for a minute.

> ***Philippians 4:19; But my Lord shall supply all your needs according to his riches in glory by Jesus Christ.***

One particular year, I was struggling with the payment of my house rent and I was seven months behind in debt. During a Holy Ghost service, the General Overseer of the Redeemed Christian Church of God, Pastor Enoch Adeboye had given a Word of Knowledge about some people who were in debt and that God would miraculously clear the debt. I smiled quietly but thought in my heart that he clearly couldn't be referring to me. A few weeks after this prophecy, the landlord arrived with a young man who he introduced as the new landlord. He told me that he had sold the house and since I am indebted, I shouldn't bother to pay anymore but requested that I move out within a week and hand over the keys to the new landlord. I felt more frustrated than ever after they left. It would have been far easier to find money and pay up the debt and stay on rather than to go looking for more than twice that amount as down payment on rent for a new apartment. This arrangement would disrupt and compound my life further. Where was the money going to come from anyway?

My son, who was about six years of age, looked on helplessly. My first impulse was to visit a man of God the following day to pray for me for God's intervention in the matter. I had just one week. The man of God had a program in one of the parishes of the Redeemed Christian Church of God. Unfortunately, all appointments to see the man of God were cancelled but he would only attend the program and leave thereafter. The program turned out to be a praise service. I told my son that we had to dance and praise God. He pulled up his little trousers and we danced our hearts out. As I watched my son dance, I cried with joy seeing him glorifying God in such an awesome manner. After the program, we went back home. As I lay on the bed, I learnt that the new landlord was around and wanted to see me. "Why can't he just allow the seven days to pass?" I said exasperated. Reluctantly I went out to see him and he came with a young lady who happened to be his wife. I thought I knew his mission. I did not.

> *Can a woman forget her sucking child that*
> *she should not have compassion on the son of*
> *her womb? Yea, they may forget, yet I will not*
> *forget thee. (Isaiah 49:15)*

The man did not get into any long conversation. He asked me to keep the house and at a later date, he would come over to discuss the rent. The seven months' rent was wiped off. And so the word of God that came from the lips of His son, Pastor Enoch Adeboye came to pass. God did not allow my son and I to become homeless. This is one of the numerous ways He was showing up in those extremely dark times. He was always there even when I hadn't come to that realization.

The sight of seeing him trying to care for himself alone always broke my heart. Once, when he was two years of age, he fell ill. At about midnight, I felt his tiny hands crawling around my neck. I woke up and found his body extremely hot. I was so tired and could not get up from bed. He was shivering all over. He got down from the bed, crawled to the rest room, crawled back and struggled to lie on my body; that was when I screamed. His body was the heat of a burning lamp. I got up in a flash and dampened him with a wet towel.

People get curious and ask questions about you behind you. I always felt the pressure. My life was basically devoted to my office job and the task of parenting my child. For too long, I kept believing that my marriage to his father would still work out, so he would get the fullness of parenting that every child deserves. Year after year, I did the same things, spoke the same words, went to the same places, prayed the same prayers, cried the same tears, and had the same thought patterns. Nothing changed. Inside of me or outside, all remained the same. I had not yielded to change in character or attitude.

The burden of single parenthood shows up on all fronts, from domestic chores to social duties. You faced all matters alone, be it tasks like fixing the car, faulty electrical, plumbing. And you-name-it. Workmen tend to take undue advantage of single women, over-billing them and coming up with fictitious claims. The auto mechanic can drain a full tank of gas, take out some autoparts or replace them with disused ones knowing that an average woman doesn't know much about cars. The electrician manipulatively creates faults thereby securing repeated patronage for himself.

It was only God that kept me. I was my own driver and in no time, I also became an electrician, a mechanic of sorts, a plumber, and every other thing. I took on chores exclusive to men because I had to do them to help my son and myself out of difficult situations. On a planned trip from Lagos to my home State, Akwa Ibom State in Nigeria, a distance of about seven hundred and twenty three kilometers, the driver I had hired failed to show up at the last minute. It was New Year's Day and I had just returned from a night vigil. After waiting till around ten o'clock in the morning and there was no sign that he would show up, I got into the car and drove the distance. I got to my parents shortly before 10pm. My father almost cried. The car had gone for servicing before this trip and I had paid for everything to be checked out and put right for the trip. In the morning, we found out one of the tyres had gone down. My father was going to help with changing it when he discovered that the spare tyre was flat as well. I had travelled all that distance, part of it in the dark of nightfall without a usable spare tyre!

I did not wait for people to do things for me. One thing I knew; only God could have given me the strength for all those tasks. I watched my son grow from infancy and teenage and young adulthood. He had every cause to be an angry young man; but thankfully he is not. His father is his hero and I am never going to let him ever think otherwise. I did not hurriedly arrange or accept a "father figure" for him. He came to love his absentee father so much that he would rather hold on to their infrequent conversations on phone than have a foster father. My responsibility was point him to God as his Heavenly father.

The two most important needs of a single mother are finances and companionship and these are the areas the enemy targets with special energy. A common mistake is to go trying to prove a point to a man that is not there, or seeking revenge by plunging headlong into illicit relationships. That would only bring on a fearsome trail of demons to completely mess up a life.

God may show His mercy and guide a single mother into a good marriage. God's mercies may also in some cases, position a father figure for her children through a blameless relationship. But if a woman goes seeking a male friendship that is aimed at getting pleasurable moments for herself, she is in for a time of regret. A single mother in desperate need for love can easily fall for any man. She could become so emotionally dependent that she would shrug off any moral restraint or scriptural counsel. She could fall into the fleshly trap of cheap sex thinking she is gaining strength from it, a pair of male hands wrapped round her as she listened to romantic whispers that she has not heard for some time. But sex does not give the strength that a single mother needs to cope with her situation. Only the Word of God can fill the void and give her the strength to make it.

Financial insecurity is a major stress where a single mother has no adequate income to meet the needs of her family. Where she is not grounded on the word of God, every gift becomes s special favour that she feels obliged to show appreciation for. If she is well advised, appreciation must not lead to any ungodly compromises. She is better than her situation suggests!

> *And as Jesus passed by, he saw a man which*
> *was blind from his birth. And his disciples*
> *asked him, saying, Master, who did sin, this*
> *man, or his parents, that he was born blind?*
> *(John 9:1-2)*

People get curious for the wrong reasons. They want to know what happened to you, not because they really care about you but because they enjoy hearing reality stories that sound like fiction. Few remember that "To his own master he standeth or falleth". (Rom 14:4) Most others believe that any terrible crisis or spiritual attacks you are facing are due to some great sin in your life. They forget that Jesus suffered and died for sins He did not commit and that from God's perspective, suffering is divine preparation for miracles that are waiting to spring forth. The world is full of hasty and uninformed judgment. "Master, who did sin"? The multitude asks, readily analyzing situations they know nothing about. These are those who ferret when your heart is bleeding. "Master, who did sin"? They frivolously discuss the personal struggles of others as if they were the ultimate authority on other people's lives. Yet in the bible, we see a voyage in which a storm raged even with Jesus aboard the boat. And we see that our Lord was not perturbed about the turbulence. The storm was subject to Him and He expected His frightened disciples to know better than to think He would ever let them suffer a shipwreck. Are you not shocked at Jesus answer to the inquisitive multitude that wanted to know whose sin was behind the blind man's sightless condition? Jesus made it clear that it is neither the man nor his parents "but that the works of God should be made manifest in him". Case closed. The depth of God's wisdom will always render the opinions of self-righteous critics and judges irrelevant.

God's purpose is always greater and deeper than man's ruthless thoughts and assumptions. The multitude cannot see the journey, they cannot see the preparation, and they cannot even feel the presence of God behind the turmoil. I had heard the Word, and I was liberated. I began to thank God for the opportunity and strength He gave to me to go through all I did even though it had not been my personal choice.

Waking up some mornings, I would remember the deliverance sessions I had been through. These were back in the days of utmost desperation. One was seeking signs and wonders; and prayer houses were here and there that thrived on the dramatic to captivate the gullible. I would be forcefully pushed to the floor and held down to prove that the power of God was in manifestation. I remember the counseling sessions where I would be asked to bring money for emergency prayers to be offered at the 'mountaintop' for me. Lies, lies, absolute and disastrous lies. Surely there is more to God than charlatans have made of His love for His children.

There are people who should never have seen my tears. Thankfully, I am in a position today to reflect on the lessons I learnt from those errors. God is perfect and true. And there is easy, direct and uncomplicated access to Him through His Son, Jesus Christ who died for all of us. Anyone who seeks Him in spirit and truth will find Him. His written word in the bible is a sure guide for the humble and trusting. Nobody should be deceived by the works of men. God is not in the gimmicks man orchestrates to his own ends.

> *That I may know Him, and the power of his resurrection, and the fellowship of his sufferings, being made conformable unto his death; (Philippians 3 :10)*

I yearned for Him, to know His ways and please Him. It did not matter anymore if I had no male voice to welcome me home. It did not matter if I had no one to share my deepest feelings with. It did not matter if I stayed all alone on a hospital bed with my son. Nothing else mattered. I was ready to serve God and tell the world about Him.

A request I repeatedly made was that God should make me a vessel in His hand; and that until He finished with me, He should not let me go. Situations came that demanded my walking in love. I started maturing in obedience and absolute sensitivity to the Holy Spirit. Nobody but God had an idea where I was going. But God knew. He was ordering my steps.

I came to a point of total and complete surrender to the Lordship of my Lord and Saviour, Jesus Christ, a point at which I asked and meant it that only His will be done in my life. I had begun to focus on the good and I got back my enthusiasm and turned deaf ears to what anyone had to say or would say.

There is tremendous power in a woman who has found herself alone with God, shouldering responsibilities that she ought to share with her husband. She draws strength from God or her family falls. The answer is not in running around, looking for another man or in dwelling in what has been, what should have been and what should be. It is knowing that God is ever present and that He longs to carry the burden with you and give you a brighter future.

I had received the inner strength to begin to birth that which had been deposited in me in spite of my circumstances. There are some who believe that a strong woman is one who has a "powerful" husband by her side, a woman who is measured by beauty and frequent appearances at high society functions, or a woman with a multi-million dollar job or business empire, or another with high social standing and international connections. But in the Kingdom, the yardstick is different. The single mother's strength is defined by her virtues and character. Her sense of duty and obedience to authority, her loyalty in service and her faithfulness in the face of calamity and chaos are defining qualities. Her greatest strength is an implicit trust in God and the confidence that He will see her through any difficult situation.

For me, a great and effectual journey had begun. It would be a journey of consecration and dedication. A journey of complete and total surrender. A journey from which I would not be distracted by fleshly desires and empty words of men. A journey that would establish God's word for my life as an indisputable and everlasting testimony.

Thank you Jesus.

CHAPTER 19

THE UNFORGETABLE ALTARS

And the Lord appeared unto Abram, and said, Unto thy seed will I give this land: and there builded he an altar unto the Lord, who appeared unto him. (Genesis 12:7)

Abraham built an altar to commemorate his encounter with God. Other notable Patriarchs in the Old Testament built altars as a reminder of God's protection, deliverance and His promises. These altars remained in place for years and those who erected them returned thereto from time to time to pray and worship God. These altars were a memorial to them and their descendants that God and no one else was their life and only Source. They were reminders to posterity that if God did it before, He sure would do it again. They were visible physical structures that enabled men to remain firmly rooted in faith.

An Altar is a place of spiritual encounter. By the mercies of Calvary, an altar is no more only the physical structures in our places of worship. It is our heart, the very centre of our being. God wants us to maintain our heart as an altar of His worship, a reminder of the miraculous deliverances of the past, His supernatural interventions and healing, His merciful provisions and the works of love that His unseen hands had done in our lives.

I went back in time to thank and praise God for all that He had done for me. It made me realize how much of His favour I had taken for granted for so long. I had so much to be grateful for. As I counted my blessings, my gratitude to God grew as did my faith in Him. From that point, I began to walk the path of victory and confidence. I could face any pressure and even if it seemed unbearable, I would remember the previous interventions by God, acts of divine mercy too numerous to reckon. I got my strength back, knowing that if God came through before, He would surely come through again for me. One thing He would never do is fail me. But the manner of His intervention on one occasion might be different from anything He had done in the past. His mercies are new every morning.

> **Bless the Lord, O my soul: and all that is**
> **within me, bless his holy name. Bless the Lord,**
> **O my soul, and forget not all his benefits.**
> **(Psalm 103:1-2)**

It is extremely impossible for me to chronicle the blessings of God upon my life considering how numerous and variegated they have been. Can I even count the many near-death experiences that I have been delivered from?

Meditating on these things, one realizes with shock how ungrateful one had been. A life of obsessions is a life of worries. When we are obsessed with the issues of our life, they grow bigger than us because we are failing to see, recognize and appreciate God's helping hand for which we ought to glorify and thank Him. God was reshaping my life and nothing else should have mattered to me. Even factors that were seemingly negative were all part of the process.

I took stock of my life, starting right from my childhood at my grandparents' home. Every experience of note that I could recall, I dutifully handed over to God, thanking and praising Him. The bible makes it clear that everything works together for good to them that love God. I praise God for the good and the bad, everything He has enabled me to go through. I thank Him that there was no "microwave" miracle in all those circumstances, just His steady assuring presence that has built me up as a sanctuary of His eternal praise. I thank Him even for closed doors and I bless Him sincerely for the part everybody has played in my life. Each and everybody's role was taking me to my destiny.

God's goodness had always been there in my life. I recall a childhood incident that occurred one morning in my grandparents' house. I was playing and running about, a long chewing stick in my mouth. About to dash into a room, I did not realize the door behind the curtain was locked. The chewing stick rammed into the door and went right through my throat. Blood, blood, blood!!! But it is four decades of that incident, and I can still sing.

Oh, how ungrateful I had been! God has been faithful, keeping me in spite of everything. He was with me in my primary, secondary and university days. He was my protector in my numerous trips by air and land especially during the university days and National Youth Service Corps year and in endless travels as a bank employee. Twice I have been in near plane crash and twice in near fatal car crashes. Thrice, I had been attacked by armed robbers at gun-point. God has seen me through some very hard times.

On more than two occasions, I ignorantly signed up into some wrong relationships that almost cost me my life. But God did not allow me to die so cheaply. He wants me to fulfill His purpose for my life. The little girl child that walked several kilometers of a forest pathway in the middle of night on the eve of her school admission interview was naïve and ignorant. But with her is the God of all creation and Lord of hosts.

Who forgiveth all thine iniquities; who healeth all thy diseases; (Psalm 103:3)

A changed life is a great miracle. You become a vessel in which the Holy Spirit dwells. When I look back at my previous unsaved state, I thank God for the miracle He has wrought in me. The physical afflictions that the enemy threw at me had seemed endless and inescapable at different points. But God delivered me from them all. I had to go under the knife a couple of times, due to health challenges. What right have I to have survived the general anaesthesia as many times as I did.

In my National Youth Service Corp posting,(a scheme set up by the Nigerian government to involve Nigerian graduates in nation building) I suffered a food poisoning episode that landed me in hospital to be drip-fed with heavy doses of antibiotics. Discharged a few days later, I promptly resumed as if nothing had had happened and as if the power to live belonged to me.

Sometime in 1998, I was diagnosed with malaria and given a dose of drugs by injection as prescribed by the doctor. The following day, my whole body was covered with chicken pox. It was an alarming sight, and I was kept in isolation. Healing came in days and the attack left no single mark on my body.

The cessation of my employment in 2006 meant the automatic termination of free medical services for me and my son in the approved hospitals. To the glory of God, my son and I have not had any serious ailment that would necessitate unaffordable medical expenses. God had been faithful and I thank Him.

> ### *Who redeemeth thy life from destruction; who crowneth thee with loving kindness and tender mercies; (Psalm 103:4)*

The birth of my son in the most awful place is still very fresh in my consciousness. If his survival and mine were not an act of God's loving kindness and tender mercies, then nothing else would ever qualify as such. My baby had no defects and didn't die in the harrowing process of his delivery. I pulled through and I am still alive to declare the goodness of the Lord in the land of the living.

I remember my harrowing experience at Hotel Excelsior in London with Mr. Obiakor and how God delivered me.

When my son was about four years old, I took him on a road trip to my home state. On our return, I discovered that my son's stomach was distended. His regular paediatrician then was a doctor that was not retained by my employer, his charges being perceptibly higher than average. It was to him I would have taken my child to but I didn't have enough cash and the fuel in my car dipped far below the reserve. So I headed to a hospital that my employer retained, one of the best at that time. A lady paediatrician there examined him and recommended that a surgery be performed the following morning. "For what"? I asked. She said my son had gone into "shock" (whatever that meant) and needed urgent surgery. I protested but the doctor stood her ground. An injection was presently administered to him (the first time since he was born) and the admission processes were quickly concluded. I became very uncomfortable and I knew suddenly that I should get out of that hospital immediately. So I told the hospital authority that I needed to fetch someone who will stay with us in the hospital. I was requested to leave my son behind but I resisted. I drove with him to far away Victoria Island in Lagos to see his regular Paediatrician, and refrained from divulging what had just transpired in the other hospital. After examining him, the professor said that there was air in his stomach and I needed to purchase some peppermints that he could suck and pass out the air. This I did as we headed back home. And as I drove into my compound, the car stopped. The fuel tank had gone dry. And my son's stomach had gone flat. Was God faithful and did I remember to thank Him?

On my way to work one morning in 1995 in, with my son and nanny in the car, a sudden explosion shattered the window of my car. Out of fear, I accelerated and sped on to a safe distance. I was in absolute shock and we were all trembling as we scrambled out of the car. What could it have been? A gun shot? No one could tell. The driver's window was shattered was. But none of us was hurt. God kept me to praise Him.

After my National Youth Service program, I had travelled back to my alma mater university to process my transcripts. On my way back to Lagos, the driver unknowingly crossed a rail track, unaware that a train was coming! We were momentarily transfixed inside the car, looking death in the face as the car shook uncontrollably. It felt like some powerful electrocution force but somehow, we made it across the rail, missing the onrushing train by only a hair's breath as it sped by. I find it hard to explain that experience. How could I ever take this God for granted? He had done so much, too much. I realized now that but for His mercies, I would have been squashed out a long time ago. That the hand of God alone, has kept me right from my mother's womb is worthy of my eternal service of the Most High.

One late night in 1997 after work, I was going home in a hired cab. The car smashed into another vehicle and I was rescued and rushed to a hospital. I had sustained minor injuries and my tongue was lacerated. I was in that hospital for about a week before I got discharged. To the glory of God, I had healed quickly and the tongue that the enemy wanted to destroy was preserved to sing God's praises. I wish I could tell it all.

February Tuesday 16, 2010 - The Redeemed Christian Church of God had its annual thirty day fasting. I had just returned from the evening service and was very hungry. On getting home, I lit the gas cooker to cook dinner. There was no electricity so the taps were dry. I had my kegs of purchased water in their usual line in the balcony. I needed some water so I went to bring a keg of water into the kitchen. But for no reason that I knew about, I kept hesitating pouring the said water into the bucket. The burning gas was roaring into a fiery blaze. I had mistakenly carried a keg of petrol into the kitchen!

What about the innumerable deliverance from spiritual attacks? The enemy was relentless but God was faithful. Talking about my experiences in this realm would be like giving the enemy some publicity but in every battle that raged against me, the Almighty gave me the victory. The attacks were ferocious but God was always there. And for this, I give Him the due praise.

In a semi conscious state one night as I was on the bed, a woman came to lie beside me, I struggled to get up and on gaining full consciousness, I realized that the half part of my body was paralyzed. With much difficulty, I began to plead the blood of Jesus. I did so for quite some time, then normalcy returned. Who else but Jesus spared my life, who else but He who knows the devices of the enemy and can make them of no effect? By getting myself to sit down with God, and study His word, I obtained a firmer understanding of what I was really facing. I received strength to confront these satanic fortresses and powers. I vow to praise my God forever.

I have heard of women who lost their sights and health when their emotional life was terribly disrupted. Some have ended up in suicide, unwisely terminating their destinies. Some others become emotional wrecks and mentally incapacitated. Some have aged faster and lost the will to live. I do not take credit for my survival. Only God deserves the Praise!

God made me whole and my spirit was healed also. I stopped complaining about life and began to give praises to God. I came to appreciate and love life. I realized that if I was not careful in handling my life, the enemy would continue his assignment even after I had stopped breathing, I reversed his machinations against me by singing the praises of God in my mouth and heart.

These are the altars that I carry in my heart and they will be there forever reminding me of God's faithfulness and mercy upon my life and family. These alters remind me that if He was there for me, He will still be merciful and I have no reason to be afraid.

My life has been full of the acts of God. But it became more glorious when I yielded to His guidance. I was longing to know His ways and He began to lead me step by step and He showed me great mercies every step of the way. He forgave my numerous failings and led me back to

His love. Thank God He is not man. He soothed my pain, my hurts and yearnings. He spoke into the damaged areas of my being and healed me. He took away my judgments. When I was desperate and seeking answers everywhere and anywhere, He remembered the blood of Jesus and forgave me. When He gave clear instructions regarding certain relationships and I disobeyed, He was merciful.

There are so many things I cannot express in writing. But when I began to recollect all the good things God had done for me, I gleefully danced and praised Him. And there is much more that He has done that I have not remembered, things I have taken for granted, things I thought I deserved and things I presumptuously took as rightfully mine.

For this God is our God, forever and ever. He will be our guide unto death. (Psalm 48 :14)

I vow to love, praise and serve Him forever.

CHAPTER 20

THE SEIGE IS OVER

My people are destroyed for lack of knowledge.
(Hosea 4 :6)

The death of Jesus was not in vain. I had come to understand this spiritual truth and I was no longer in bondage to anything or anyone. I decided to put everything I knew into my life so that the course of my life will experience a spiritual re-awakening. I settled in my mind that in order to fulfill my purpose in life, I must abide in the presence of God. Even when I had received powerful prophetic utterances from genuine men of God, I must get up and play my part in prayers or God's promises to me might go unfulfilled. God is not unfaithful, but He has fully equipped us with knowledge and revelation resources to enter into our inheritance. That is why we cannot afford to hand over our lives to fellow mortals. The enemy has been on a violent rampage right from the fall of man. He has ordained his cohorts to infiltrate the body of Christ. To depend completely on the prayers of other men without doing your part is the basest form of life a Christian can ever live. God wants each and everyone to have a close and personal walk with Him.

> *For the Lord had made the host of the Syrians*
> *to hear a noise of chariots, and a noise of*
> *horses, even the noise of a great host: and they*
> *said one to another, Lo, the king of Israel hath*

> *hired against us the kings of the Hittites, and*
> *the kings of the Egyptians, to come upon us.*
> *Wherefore they arose and fled in the twilight,*
> *and left their tents, and their horses, and their*
> *asses, even the camp as it was, and fled for*
> *their life. (2 Kings 7:6-7)*

Israel was powerless against the Syrian army. The Israelites suffered the worst degradation in the long siege by the invading Syrians. However, God, in His mercy had intervened but they did not know.

A siege is one of the worst satanic devices. Only Jesus brings a siege to an end. No man, no power and no magic or method can withstand the assaults of satan in these times without the power in the name and the blood of Jesus. God had to orchestrate and magnify the footsteps of the four lepers and caused the Syrian army to hear the noise that sent them fleeing in terror. And the Israelites "spoiled the tents of the Syrians". So the Word of God spoken through Prophet Elisha came to an undisputed fulfillment.

I sat down for years thinking I was waiting on God to come through for me. Year after year, I found myself chorusing some yearly clichés such as "This is my year of fulfillment, this is my year of restoration, this is my year of supernatural breakthrough ..." And painfully, as each year passed, I wondered aloud if I really knew what I was saying because there was no manifestation in any of the declarations I mouthed and there were no positive changes. At the beginning of each year, I would intensify my prayers because I thought I did not pray enough the year before.

It was either something was wrong with God or there was something terribly wrong with me. But there was something painfully wrong with me. Not God! God had been waiting on me to rise up and begin to enjoy the spoils from the camp of the enemy but I was still seated. I thought the siege would be over when I would be handed over a contract worth millions of US dollars or a job that would take me to all the continents of the world. Sadly, God's ways are not man's ways. Like the Israelites, I did not know the siege was over although things had changed in the realm of the spirit in my favour. I thought I would have the physical manifestations of the declarations I had chorused. I was still praying to God to intervene.

I believe at the point when the lepers went to the city, the Israelites must have intensified their prayers. They had become used to so much suffering and did not believe that the siege would ever be over or so near to its end.

I began to pay attention to the nudgings in my heart concerning what my Heavenly father had called me to do. Occasionally, Jesus would be merciful to send a word to me regarding all that I had in my heart. I could not catch the needful passion. I wanted God to move first before I took any step. Amazingly, my ministry and everything I would do for Him began to unfold in the midst of those challenges. As far back as 2009, I had started putting some things down on paper, trying to write a book as led. But I wasn't committed and the desire soon fizzled out.

December 16 2010. 4:41 am. I received this revelation amongst others at a time that the battle for my destiny was so intense. At that time, I had received several other revelations about my life, some of them giving me express instructions as to what I must do. I was learning to be led and willingly returned to God in prayer over any mistakes I made in following His instructions. A letter is brought to me. The name of the person that sends this letter literally means "almighty" or 'the biggest'. The ink colour is blue and it is the most amazingly beautiful handwriting I have ever seen. Well articulated and constructively crafted, the uniqueness of that handwriting defies description. The lettering is bold and is so beautiful that I admire it for long before reading. The letter is serialized, each point stating what this sender wants to do for me. But the second point gets my attention and it was a question: **"WHAT IS YOUR MISSION STATEMENT"**? Initially, I misinterpreted the revelation but I kept praying until the Holy Spirit revealed some interesting things to me.

I am on a mission on this earth but I didn't know. I have not forgotten the handwriting and the question neither have I forgotten the promises! I started considering seriously the promptings in my heart from then on and taking bold moves to be used by Him.

At the Holy Ghost Congress in December 2013, my Father in the Lord, the General Overseer of the Redeemed Christian Church of God, Pastor Enoch Adeboye had given a Word of Knowledge. He said emphatically that for someone in the congregation, "The siege is over and the person's destiny shall be restored". I knew without a shadow of the doubt that that word was for me and I claimed it for myself and thanked God. "So now that the siege is over, what next?" I kept asking myself. I had tried to put my hands in some business ventures which didn't work. My contract job was on but it was not sufficient to settle my mounting bills. I was asking God, "What do I do for you now"?

Subsequently, after the West African Believers Conference (WAFBEC) 2014 in January, I turned to my usual morning tonic on the television. This day, it was a new series titled "Strategies for Taking a Quantum Leap". God always had a word for me in this telecast. He had been waiting, screaming for me to get up and do all He had put in my heart. I had encountered some visitations in this regard but, I did not know how to go about it. As I listened to the man of God on the television, I had spirit an urgency to get up and look for the book, 'THE SEIGE IS OVER' that was published by Pastor Enoch Adeboye several years earlier. When I eventually got it, I turned to the back cover, and these words quickly jumped at me, "Now that the siege is over, increase your scope. Enlarge your vision. Expand your coast because there is nothing to hinder you anymore."

EUREKA! This was the moment I desperately longed for, a confirmation of His go-ahead in my life. This confirmed all that the Senior Pastor was saying on the television and for a moment, I cried. I cried because, the prison had been opened a long time ago and I did nothing. My future was not in the hands of any man but God and He had preserved me and kept me for His use. The Word of God from the telecast had penetrated every part of my life and de-mystified all preconceived ideas and broken all the impossibilities and stronghold. There was a word for every area of my life that was still in darkness. I had no excuses anymore. I could recount the various visitations where God had been patiently waiting and asking me to be quick in my assignment and I kept delaying. I was so afraid and I cried. I thought I was going to die because the urgency was so frightening.

The siege was over. Sometime after this Word of Knowledge from my Father in the Lord, I had a revelation in which I saw myself behind a fortified wall. The walls were all steel and iron; nobody came in and nobody went out. It was like a prison. The keys were in the hands of some guards who were supervising the inmates. Some of the inmates were wild and dreadful. I was in there, walking about and hitting the wall, as there was no way to go out. Suddenly, I went to one of the guards and told him that I needed to go somewhere, that he should open the gate for me. He promptly opened it and as soon as I stepped out, the gate was closed and immediately I woke up. I started praising and worshipping God. My spirit was free. The siege was over. I did not have to look on the outside for expected signs. God wanted me to rise up, have the boldness and the tenacity of a lion and birth my destiny.

> *Oh that men would praise the Lord for his goodness, and for his wonderful works to the children of men! For he hath broken the gates of brass, and cut the bars of iron in sunder.*
> *(Psalm 107: 15-16)*

The siege was indeed over."

CHAPTER 21

THE ASSIGNMENT

And the angel answered and said unto her,
The Holy Ghost shall come upon thee, and the
power of the Highest shall overshadow thee:
therefore also that holy thing which shall be
born of thee shall be called the Son of God.
(Luke 1: 35

An angel had announced the birth of Jesus. The angel said "He shall be called the Son of God". The plan for man's redemption was unfolded. It would be through this seed – Jesus!

Jesus had an assignment. His assignment was to restore man back to God through His death and resurrection. John the Baptist had an assignment. He would be the forerunner of Jesus. Moses had an assignment; he had the responsibility of leading the children of Israel from Egypt to the Promised Land. Noah, Nehemiah, Rahab, Gideon, Jonah, Joshua, Jeremiah and so many others had assignments from God. And wait for this; every born again Christian has an assignment, that is the Great Commission; to take the gospel to the ends of the world. However, there are some special or specific assignments that God chooses for His children. That is why it was not just anybody that could lead the children of Israel out of Egypt. That's why the spies chose Rehab's house to hide. Rehab's house had long been chosen even when she was involved in sexual immorality.

But God hath chosen the foolish things of the world to confound the wise; and hath chosen the weak things of the world to confound the things which are mighty; And base things of the world, and things which are despised, hath God chosen, yea, and things which are not, to bring to nought things that are: That no flesh should glory in his presence (1 Corinthians 1 -27–29)

Most times God uses the unqualified, the forgotten and the despised. When He picked Moses the stutterer, Aaron the smooth talking brother was right beside Moses. Gideon was from a less prominent tribe yet He visited and gave him an assignment. Everybody cannot be General Overseer, or General Superintendent, Bishop or Pastor of a congregation. But God in His uniqueness has given us something very special to enhance the spread of the gospel of the Kingdom. And that is why there are diverse gifts. It is therefore left for every Christian to find out specifically what God requires of him or her. For example, your travails, if viewed from God's perspective, could be the pointer to your God given assignment. In the midst of the multitude of my challenges, I knew one day I would tell the story. For there are lessons people must learn, words that have not yet been spoken and songs that are yet unwritten. Another important thing to note here is that God's assignment is not necessarily glamorous. If you think it must be, ask Moses, Noah, John the Baptist or Jesus. So it is very important to be sensitive to the Spirit of God to know what exactly He has called you for and how He wants you to go about it.

And he said unto them, Take heed, and beware of covetousness: for a man's life consisteth not in the abundance of the things which he possesseth. (Luke 12:15)

Some Christians have been so carried away by material fixations that they forget that everyone of us is only passing through the earth, and that eternity holds the greater promise. We have equated spirituality with material accomplishments not minding whether the visible success is good or bad.

So we struggle, some of us trying to manipulate others. We fall into the worldly race to surpass everyone else in the bid to acquire wealth; we seek to be recognized and worshipped by men. We have confused material wealth with God's assignment. We have sold our souls to men who flaunt wealth in church, wrongly regarding them as God's appointed messiahs. Sad to observe the fate of the despised poor who are now made to feel like they are rejected by God; they are full of resorts and struggles in a bid to become what God did not purpose them to be. If you are sensitive, you sense the unhealthy competition and rivalry, all in the house of our great God. It is saddening. But that is not to say that God has not raised a lot of men and women whom He has favored with great business ideas and whom He has enabled to tap into His wealth on this earth. To His glory, several of these men and women are rightly walking with God. They refuse to sell their souls for money or fame; some of them making so much sacrifice with their resources for the kingdom of God in the scriptural and humble way. These are not the sort I am referring to here but the very type indeed that we must be praying our God to increase and multiply amongst us. The work of Missions has diminished because this type who are the major sponsors of pure church work and who give without seeking personal recognition, has reduced in number in most of our churches. Today, we crowd our churches into the comfortable urban cities and abandon the poor rural areas and trouble spots. But God's work is begging to be done everywhere. We thank God for the lives of those who heed this call.

> *For unto everyone that hath shall be given,*
> *and he shall have abundance: but from him*
> *that hath not shall be taken away even that*
> *which he hath. (Matthew 25:29)*

The revelation of this scripture completely unsettled me. God had blessed me as I have since come to recognize. I had always loved to write and to sing but I had not begun to use these gifts maximally for the Kingdom. I was not even evangelizing to bring souls into the kingdom. Fearing that I might lose my gifts, I went pleading with Jesus and promised that I would do all that He ever asked of me.

On September 15, 2012 at 4.38 and 5.58 am, I had some unique visitation concerning what my father had put in my heart to do and timing was emphasized. From this date, I had no rest anymore. I dusted up my exercise book and started to write this book. I have since then been recording notes of urgency. Over the months the tempo had increased. Spiritual experiences are so difficult to explain that oftentimes I wouldn't even attempt to push myself at all except I was led to. But there were times I would get up shaking, my pen and book in hand and crying to Jesus to help me. My thoughts, prayers and utterances began to centre around this book. I had lost my peace and quiet and could not seem to regain it except I kept writing. In my daily praise and study of God's word, I would sometimes receive flashes of inspiration. A new song would drop in my spirit and I would quickly record it on my phone. I never did sit down to think of what songs to write. They came as I meditated on God's word and as I praised and worshipped my Lord Jesus.

I had promised Him that I would do whatever He asked me to do for Him. I meant it to the letter because understanding my purpose on this earth and doing it would be my greatest fulfillment. I was sure that any further waste of time might spell doom. Even the gift of the whole world would not assuage my thirst.

CHAPTER 22

INTERPRET YOUR DREAMS AND LIFE

And it came to pass in the morning that his spirit was troubled; and he sent and called for all the magicians of Egypt, and all the wise men thereof: and Pharaoh told them his dream; but there was none that could interpret them unto Pharaoh.......... And Joseph answered Pharaoh, saying, It is not in me: God shall give Pharaoh an answer of peace. (Genesis 41:8,16)

I lacked the ability to interpret my dreams in my early Christian life. Even when a lot of those dreams were plain and direct. I just couldn't figure out any significance beyond their movie-like experience. I sought in bookshops and found books on the interpretation of dreams. I also sought help in interpretation from people. But I got little satisfaction in these efforts. To the contrary, I was often left more confused by them.

With so much happening in quick succession and my life spiraling downwards at that time, it looked as if the enemy was having the upper hand. I had not yet learnt to master my life, emotions and environment. I had not yet developed that inner strength to resist and overcome demonic arrows. Until I sat down to the word of God, I was just like Pharoah who sent for the magicians by virtue of his position; and would go looking for people who more often than not gave wrong and misleading interpretations. On the few occasions that some of the interpretations made sense, the recommendations that followed were mostly ungodly. The whole situation was getting increasingly frustrating and if for any reason I got fascinated by any of those ungodly prescriptions, I would suffer life-threatening consequences.

Spiritual things hardly work by or follow age, position, fame or experience. They work according to one's relationship with the Holy Spirit. Your depth of understanding of God's word and your ability to exercise faith in it determines your spiritual direction and altitude. I had picked up a lot from the Spirit and there was one thing I did; I talked about them. I don't blame Pharoah for threatening to kill off the soothsayers who couldn't render a credible interpretation of his dreams. Like him and King Nebuchadnezzar much later, I had been frustrated a thousand times with misinterpretation of serious dreams. In King Nebuchadnezzar's case, he even forgot the dream and threatened to kill the wise men if they couldn't tell him both the dream and its meaning. You wouldn't wish to be one of those wise men, would you? The true wisdom that no flesh could match lay with the young Joseph, a spirit-filled lad imprisoned on false charges.

My situation changed as I started gaining wisdom from the Word of God and spending time with the Holy Spirit. The most amazing revelations of my dreams and visions began to dawn on me. Almost all the major events of my life which came to me in those seasons were in the Word of God. It was a marvel as even the dates and years of key events in my life were shown to me in the Word of God. Future events were revealed to me with so much clarity that I came to the perfect conviction that God indeed is the author of the Holy Book. The prophetic books mirrored my life and showed me some very specific dreams and revelations that I had had over the years. That I found myself in the word of God is a wonder that will forever blow my mind.

I believe today that everything that happens in the life of a Christian is for a purpose. It is left for us to decode that purpose. One snare that every Christian must avoid is carnal wisdom of friends and relations influencing their choices and decisions. Psalm 1 declares that " Blessed is the man that walketh not in the counsel of the ungodly..." Dreams and their godly interpretations are special and helpful divine gifts. But what is most important, in whatever way God speaks to you, it is to hear him well in order to decode the direction of your life. Unbridled obsession with dream could render you vulnerable to manipulation if you fail to be discerning and to fight your spiritual battles on your knees.

I never could make any progress in resolving my spiritual issues until I began to treat the things of God with utmost sacredness. For example, I studied to be quiet as the bible enjoins us all. I no longer talk much apart from normal courtesies, I hardly engage in long discussions except I am led to.

A Christian will manifest the awesome power of God if he uses his gifts for God's pleasure. Just consider Joseph and Daniel who had an excellent spirit. Both were able to solve difficult riddles for Pharoah and Nebuchadnezzar respectively. Today the world is looking for the Josephs and Daniels in the Kingdom. Christians are the light of the world and the salt of the earth and until we cooperate with God and allow Him to use us for signs and for wonders, the world would not take us seriously. The challenges of this world are waiting to be unlocked by Christians. Kings of the earth are desperate to get answers to questions that power and money cannot provide.

The surest way God reveals himself to his children is through His Word and every answer to life lies therein. He chooses to manifest as he pleases but He never contradicts His Word. God's children have various ways of receiving revelation, instructions, or directions from God. Some have angelic visitations, direct rhema from His Word or dreams, visions, trances, etc. The important thing is to know what to do with any God-given revelation.

I do not claim to have become a master in interpreting dreams. But one thing I started doing after my deliverance was to pray about my dreams whether I understood them or not. I would nullify the negative ones by the blood of Jesus. I have learnt too much to ever allow any dream to pass without the searchlight of my prayers. In the days of ignorance, I allowed too many things to pass over my head and the result was losses and adversities. But since I learnt to watch and pray, and to understand the significance of dreams the pieces of my life's puzzle have come together little by little.

I cannot tell why God in His wisdom got me into journaling of my dreams since March 1996. What I am happy about is that they have since become my reference points in prayer. It was this "archive" that I visited to get my bearings for the fight to destroy the fortresses that the enemy had built around me. It was hard work. As I sat back with the Word and analyzed each dream, I could not but thank God for His protection over my life and family. The enemy's attacks were massive but nothing happened that had not been shown to me long beforehand. It was God's grace that even though I was rather late in learning how to apply it, I am still alive today. God in His infinite mercy gave me another chance. The most important thing is that I no longer live in ignorance and the mission of the enemy was completely truncated.

> *If it had not been the Lord who was on our*
> *side, now may Israel say; If it had not been the*
> *Lord who was on our side, when men rose up*
> *against us: (Psalm 124:1)*

Now, I have a lot in my life to deal with. My night hours had become my watching moments.

Dreams and visions are however not the only means you could get to know what is happening around you. There is much to discern in people's words and actions and signs are forever speaking in body language and various happenings around us. For the observant, God can use any of these things to point one to a future event. One thing every Christian should know is that God is good and loving. He does not like His children to be ambushed by the enemy or to be taken by surprise. He reveals things before they happen.

> ***The secret of the Lord is with them that fear him; and he will shew them his covenant. (Psalm 25:14)***

God is still in the business of granting His children a preview of coming events. It is our own business to decode His revelation whether they come as dream, vision, trance or other signs. Failing to heed his divine promptings brings a lot of regret. Had I died, the popular bible passage -"The Lord gives, the Lord takes away..." would have been on everybody's lips. Or, to comfort themselves, some would say – "He takes the best."

No! God is not in the business of terminating destinies. It is the devil that does that if he is allowed a quarter. The sooner a Christian grasped this revelation, the better as it will position him to fight for his destiny. I have discovered that life becomes more interesting when you face your issues with prayer unto victories in Christ. Your ability to confront issues fearlessly gives you the edge and in no time despair, doubts and other weaknesses that lead to failure and frustrations flee from you. I once watched a young bus driver in a street brawl. He had been stripped naked but he kept fighting so much that he attracted the attention of law-enforcement agents. But nothing they did could stop the wild lad as he continued fighting. Passersby ran for their lives because it was getting very unsafe. Boldly written at the back of his bus were three words; LIFE IS WAR! One could figure from that motto why the young man kept fighting so ferociously. I meditated on that episode for months until the truth hit me. Yes! Every Christian is involved in spiritual WARFARE! It is such a relentless battle, the enemy employing every weapon and act of wickedness to steal, kill and destroy those who do not know their place in Christ. As Christians, we have a special privilege in that we go into this battle knowing that victory has already been won for us and all we need to do is claim that victory by putting on the whole armour of God and standing on the Rock of our Salvation. The battle of life is not for the weak or fearful; it is for the strong and faithful for whom failure is not an option.

One great lesson I have learnt is to take everything to God in prayer. As I developed intimacy with the Holy Spirit and allowed the Word of God to be the compass in my life, I gained capacity to decode events. I urge my fellow Christians to rise up as the real supermen we are in Christ. The world out there is awaiting the manifestation of the sons of God.

CHAPTER 23

THE GARMENT OF PRAISE

Sing, O barren, thou that didst not bear; break forth into singing, and cry aloud, thou that didst not travail with child: for more are the children of the desolate than the children of the married wife, saith the Lord. Enlarge the place of thy tent, and let them stretch forth the curtains of thine habitations: spare not, lengthen thy cords, and strengthen thy stakes; for thou shalt break forth on the right hand and on the left; and thy seed shall inherit the Gentiles, and make the desolate cities to be inhabited. (Isaiah 54 : 1–3)

My Catholic beliefs and orientation had made Christ look distant and out of reach until I accepted Jesus as my personal Lord and Saviour. Adversity had presented God as a distant, disciplined dictator who sat in heaven to whip and punish His children when they missed it. So I felt guilty and could not even praise Him with love and understanding. The fear of continued chastisement ruled my faint-hearted approach to God.

At the time, I didn't even understand spiritual warfare or the power in praise of God. I saw prayer as a gift that God had given to some people alone. Even after I gave my life to Christ, I still treated prayer only peripherally. I did commence praying a bit more on getting born again, but it was a struggle and I never enjoyed it. Little did I know that God had His plans and that the challenges of my life would eventually teach me the discipline of closet moments and the unbelievable joys in genuine, heartfelt prayers of a worshipful soul. I came to know that Jesus has paid for all my sins and tribulations. I came to know that there are wicked spirits and dark powers contending with my destiny. I also came to understand that unless I arose and exercised my authority, as a believer and took control over what seemed to control my life, I wouldn't experience the Christian victory.

I was soon singing praises to God from my heart knowing He has been God in my life. There are several promises in the Word of God that suited my life. I settled in my heart that, in whatever situation I find myself, praising God would become a part of my life. Then I came to know the truth was His grace and mercy. I had not given God His place in my life. I neither claim to know every verse from Genesis to Revelation nor to pray, sing praises and worship God all hours of the day. The fact is, God ordered His servants into my life through the books they wrote, programs they organized, messages they preached and the songs they sang. And I had to humble myself and I learnt what God was using them to teach me. It didn't matter anymore what I went through to get to this point; if I had to go through it a thousand times, I would praise God even more.

> *And he took him a potsherd to scrape himself*
> *withal; and he sat down among the ashes.*
> *(Job 2:8)*

The picture of ashes is the picture of desperation, sorrow, losses, disappointment, helplessness, brokenness, bitterness, anguish, grief, disappointment and death. Job had been reduced to nothing. No one can imagine the depth of his grief. When one goes through anything near the kind of calamity Job endured, hardly would there be talk of praising God. Nobody told Job to worship God when he did in the immediate aftermath of his total devastation. The bitter complaints would only come at a much later point. But clearly, at his first hearing of the terrible news that everything he owned in human and material wealth had perished, what he did was worship God, a deep spiritual act that told volumes of the kind of man Job was. God who saw that must have sworn by His own precious name that even if Job turned around later to accuse Him, the man would be fully restored.

The reason the devil attacks us is to steal the praises of God from our hearts and lips especially during moments of crises and pain. At such times, all that the human eyes can see is the confusion. Only God's grace can help you to worship Him in such difficult moments. I learnt valuable lessons about life and the true worship of God through the difficulties I passed through in my own life. Today, I have much to thank God for and my worship of Him is real. I candidly testify that I cannot wish for a better life.

> *Which none of the princes of this world knew;*
> *for had they known, they would not have*
> *crucified the Lord of glory. (1 Corinthians 2:8)*

All that the enemy had orchestrated was to keep me focused on the wrong things and cause me to pursue those things which are detrimental to my salvation and destiny. Now, I knew better. Right in the centre of the negative things that had once held me bound, as I present them before God in praise, I see the light of His glorious power swallowing up all the darkness, illuminating my mind, pouring into my spirit the joy I could not explain. Just like blind Bartimeaus cast away his garment, rose and came to Jesus, in my moments with Jesus as I worship Him, I don't have any sense of loss or grief. I wear no mournful garment or tearful countenance. I don't remember the wrongs done, or the ill words said. I take everything to Him in worship, I take everything to Him in praise and I leave them there. I have refused to give up on God and I refuse to give up on myself. I do not answer every call or try to kill every fly that passes any longer, neither do I join every arguments or every social circle nor do I respond to every criticism or answer every question. Nothing and no one else but God deserves such special attention.

The battle of life is fierce and the most potent weapon to defeat the enemy is praise of God. Every bit of my experiences has helped to define my character. God dealt with my every weakness and stripped me of crutches and dependence so that I can make Him my only Source and be that which he had ordained me to be. The battles may not be completely over but He has equipped me and given me the power to prevail over the enemy. This is my resurrection! My priorities are all changed. Things and people I felt I couldn't do without have all faded out. Even at the risk of being hard on myself, I am completely sold on self-discipline because I have seen a bigger and better picture.

By God's grace, I have broken every allegiance that took my attention away from God. I destroyed, returned or gave away material gifts of questionable import and others I didn't buy with my money. I made restitutions wherever I was led to and cut every tie that had held me bound. I am loving this experience of travelling light, unburdened by material lusts, just looking unto Jesus. A number of times, the hedge around me has been broken through careless interaction and utterances especially. With the enemy running wild, I am thankful to God for His covering grace. I have also learnt to be more watchful, more discerning, and more prayerful. I have a new life, a life without any baggage and I thank God for giving me the opportunity to go through all that has brought me thus far.

> *For his anger endureth but a moment; in his favour is life; weeping may endure for a night, but joy cometh in the morning. (Psalm 30:5)*

It no longer matters how long I stayed in the crib. What matters is that I saw a new day and embraced it. And death lost its power over me.

One of the most profound statements that has given me so much strength is from a sermon titled "Receiving Strength to Face the Test" one of the telecasts in the programme, **Insights** *for* **Living**. The Senior Pastor said …." *And nothing is too late. The bible says that Sarah, even though she was past the age judged Him faithful …. In the spirit realm, time cannot erase*

145

the Word of God. The gifts and callings of God are without repentance. The fact that you did not get it right ten years ago …. so long as you are alive, you are only alive because God can still fulfill his Will through you. So don't say my time is past, as long as you are there, the promise of God can still come to pass. So don't be too proud to make the adjustments….

These words have refused to leave my consciousness! In my sleep, I hear them! In my waking moments, I hear them! In my journey to destiny, I hear them! It is not late, it is not late, the Holy Spirit whispers. Such comforting words! The Master of time, The Force behind every breath, The Merciful has been at work in my life. I owe my entire life to Him alone. I am assured of a fresh beginning. It does not matter how many times I blew away my previous chances, God can still be trusted and He will do the impossible in my life.

New Shoes…. New Shoes…. my song! It is no longer an echo. There are no limitations anymore. I have found my voice. It was with me, has always been and will forever be. It is the voice that praises and worships the Almighty God for what He has done, for what He is doing and for what He will do. The God of the entire Universe, The Regulator of every second of creation, The God that Preserves for Greatness.

CHAPTER 24

CONCLUSION

No child defines the course of his life. Similarly, there are choices and decisions that will not be made by you. For example you cannot choose your parents, brothers and sisters. And no one except the creator Himself can predict accurately the events that will shape and actualize the ultimate path and purpose of a living soul. If it were possible, we would all write out nicely every phase of our lives and make it one long, beautiful story without dark seasons. But herein lies the infinite wisdom of God, the creator of man and author of his destiny. Even if one catches glimpses of one's future as Joseph did, attaining it is not always guaranteed or predictable because trials and challenges could throw one off-balance unless one is firmly rooted in Christ. Job could not argue with God and win a right to divine vindication on the basis of self-righteousness. We cannot arrogate righteousness and its concomitant armour of protection to ourselves as Righteousness is of God. Job's presumptuous human arguments would give way to a deeper understanding of the mind of God at the later part of his travails. He would realize in spiritual maturity that he had earlier on spoken without any understanding.

> ### *Who is this that darkeneth counsel by words*
> ### *without knowledge? (Job 38:2).*

If I could influence or alter my destiny in any way to suit my carnal desires, I would have done so in the undue haste and ignorance of an average girl child. It has taken a painful journey to bring me to the point of realization and joyful acceptance of God's purpose for my life. I have surrenderd my will completely and totally to Him. And I thank Him that He did not grant me things of the flesh that I desperately wanted in the past. I thank Him for doors He shut that could have led to my destruction.

The trials and temptations that came my way may have been part of the process to make me who God wants me to be. All I have gone through are "light afflictions" which God allowed to work for me "a far and exceeding weight of glory" (2Cor 4:17) No matter what other affliction that may show up, I will still praise him with a perfect heart and joyful spirit that He has granted me.

The Almighty has prepared me to walk with Him and obey Him to the very end. He has called me and set me apart for Himself. Wherever He leads, I will follow. Every past mistake or misstep is a blessing in disguise as God has turned it all into an opportunity to purge and bring out the best in me for His service. The process of refining is ongoing and the grace of God is sufficient for this walk.

It doesn't matter anymore what comes or goes. It doesn't matter who stays or leaves; there is a race to win or lose. I have chosen to win. That is all that matters to me. The word of God is my compass. The race by Him is a call to complete obedience and humility not the hot pursuit of material comfort. It is a call to sanctification and absolute purity. It is a call to a closer walk with the Holy Spirit, to do only his Will, not mine. The enemy has never wearied of attacking God's chosen vessels. But he remains a defeated foe. I am no more captive to desperation and anxious moments. I am completely delivered from fear. I have absolute confidence that my future is bright and I have been called to be an integral part of God's work on earth. For this, I am eternally grateful.

One thing have I desired of the Lord, that
will I seek after; that I may dwell in the house
of the Lord all the days of my life, to behold

the beauty of the Lord, and to enquire in his temple. (Psalm 27: 4)

I want to know Him. I want to know His ways. I want to please Him and stand in awe of Him. I want to serve Him with everything in me and with all that I have. And when my life on this earth is over, He will welcome me home and say "well done, my covenant child".

As for the dreams, according to Mark Rutland in his Book DREAM, he wrote that "…Dreams do not explain the future; the future will finally explain the dream".

Printed in the United States
By Bookmasters